Above the Treeline

Above the Treeline

Towards a Contemporary Spirituality

Heije Faber

ABINGDON PRESS/Nashville

ABOVE THE TREELINE
Towards a Contemporary Spirituality

Translated by John Bowden from the Dutch
Boven de boomgrens. Op weg naar een hedendaagse spiritualiteit,
published by Uitgeverij Ten Have bv, Baarn, Netherlands.

© Uitegeverij Ten Have 1987

Translation © John Bowden 1988

This book is printed on acid-free paper.

Library of Congress Cataloging-in-Publication Data

Faber, Heije, 1907–
Above the treeline.
Translation of: Boven de boomgrens.
Bibliography: p.
1. Spiritual life. I. Title.
BV4501.2.F26 1989   248.4   88-35123

ISBN 0-687-00680-5 (alk. paper)

First British edition published 1988
by SCM Press Ltd
26-30 Tottenham Road, London, N1 4BZ

U.S. edition published 1989 by Abingdon Press,
201 Eighth Ave. South, Nashville, Tennessee

MANUFACTURED BY THE PARTHENON PRESS AT
NASHVILLE, TENNESSEE, UNITED STATES OF AMERICA

CONTENTS

PREFACE

In the summer of 1984 I was invited by the Benedictine abbey in Oosterhout, Netherlands, to give a series of lectures (or perhaps they might better be called reflections or meditations) during the next winter to the monks there. I was left free to choose the subject, but it was hoped that I could say something in the area of spirituality.

I gladly accepted the invitation and during the winter of 1984-1985 I travelled to Oosterhout six times, on each occasion dealing with a particular topic during the evening and then again the following morning. As a result of my studies in connection with the psychology of religion and pastoral psychology I had been increasingly attracted by the question of the nature and possibilities of religious experience in the contemporary world. This was the question that I chose as my theme. I have come to see that this question can and must be approached in different ways. First, sociologically: the problems associated with religious experience cannot be understood unless account is taken of the profound changes in our society. Secondly, psychologically: especially as a result of psycho-analysis we have gained some insight into the way in which our religious experience is bound up with our psychological development. Thirdly, philosophically: reflection on human existence in existentialism has shown where and how philosophical perspectives crop up in it. And finally, in the framework of a reflection on spirituality: this phenomenon, which derives from Roman Catholic circles, is at present being discussed in all kinds of groups and movements; questions about religious experience cannot really be clarified apart from the discussion.

This book has grown out of the reflections that I shared with the community in Oosterhout. So in it I shall be approaching the problems of religious experience from several angles.

The book as a whole is held together by the image of a mountain climb which I undertake with my readers – as I undertook it with my audience in Oosterhout. We set out from a mountain village, through a wood, and then emerge above the treeline, where we look for our further route with a view of the summit. I should stress that it is not my intention to offer a scientific proof, but that at the same time I want to describe the way as clearly as I can. So at the end I have provided some notes to the book, which I hope may be of use to you on your journey. It is for you to judge whether in these pages about problems of religious experience – and thus about the possibilities of a contemporary spirituality – I have succeeded in writing personally without becoming didactic in a way which fails to do justice to intellectual clarity. I see this book as an attempt to show something of modern theology as a living force. I feel an affinity to much that plays a part in so-called radical theology, and that is the reason why I do not feel at home in much modern and often fashionable conservatism, which I often feel to be escapism from the more serious difficulties of our existence.

Finally, I should say that this book places considerable emphasis on the significance of community and at the same time stresses the necessity for a personal choice. Some people might ask whether this does not betray a hidden 'élitism'. While that may be true to some degree, it does not mean that we must strive to form 'élites', but that the future of our society depends on the presence of small groups of people with awareness.

Maarn

one

A View of the Summit

Many people experience their lives as a journey: we are fond of relating all the things that we encounter on our way.

In this book I see life as a mountain climb, as following a way which leads up from a valley in the direction of a summit.

The question of spirituality[1]

I have chosen this image of the mountain climb deliberately. In 1950 Martin Heidegger, the well-known German philosopher, put together a collection of articles under the title *Holzwege*.[2] To explain this title he wrote: ' "Holz" is an old German word for wood. In the wood there are ways which are usually overgrown and which suddenly come to a dead end. They are called "Holzwege". Each of them takes a different course, but all are in the same wood. Often one seems like another. But that is an illusion. Woodcutters and wardens know the ways. They know what it means to be on a "Holzweg".'

On the basis of the articles in this collection, for Heidegger, life is like being on a 'Holzweg', looking for a way in the wood. His argument is that our own ways often lead to a dead end with no way forward. The ways in our life are densely overgrown and we cannot get out of them. Human existence is difficult.

The image of the mountain climb says something different. It suggests that in our existence we can be going up a way which leads towards a summit, in other words that we can have a purpose in our lives. The journey may be difficult, but it sometimes offers new and often wide perspectives; we can climb out of the darkness of the valley into the bright and clear light near the summit.

Heidegger's book is a collection of essays. He guides the reader round the spheres of art and philosophy, science and faith, and in his tour an article on Nietzsche's remark that God is dead occupies a key position. In this book, too, I shall be offering a series of essays. You might call them reflections, meditations. There is some connection between them, a theme that holds them all together: in contrast to Heidegger's article about the death of God my theme is that of God's presence in our life.[3] It is perhaps worth indicating what I mean by this. The theme can be described as that of spirituality. We can see that there is a search for spirituality. It appears time and again in books: in reflections on pastoral care it is concerned not just with better 'techniques of communication' nor even with a profile of the identity of the modern pastor, but with his or her spirituality, inner life, faith, 'dealings' with God.

What is at issue here, in my view, is the question of the possibility (or perhaps the impossibility) of the presence of God in human existence. Let's be honest. God is usually absent. Or to put it in a much more sober way: we are far too busy for God. But things also go deeper than that: we often no longer believe in the possibility of his presence. Is he not a product of our projections? It may even be that when we are talking or reading about God, indeed sometimes in the midst of our liturgical actions, we may begin to wonder whether we are really occupied with real things. However, experience shows that something happens when God is 'present'. Our spirit – our thoughts and feelings – is then moved. We begin to realize what spirituality can mean.

Personal background

Perhaps you may wonder how I arrived at this theme. My answer is that psychological investigation of the structure of religious experience plays an important part in my professional occupation, which is pastoral psychology. One question which has been put by many people under the influence of psycho-analysis or

Marxism is whether this religious experience is based on imagination and is therefore an illusion or whether it can be authentic and genuine. We can also see a considerable decline in church membership at the present time and even a growth of unbelief. That leads to a question which many people are asking: what is happening here? Why are people abandoning their church or their belief? I have gone into this question in some of my recent books. In doing so I have discovered that the problem of the structure, the nature of underlying religious experience in the background, is of decisive importance.

For many men and women of my generation this problem also has a clear personal significance. They discovered after the war that they were also confronted with radical questions in their personal life relating to their belief and their membership of a church. John Robinson with his *Honest to God* and other books,[4] Bonhoeffer with his *Letters and Papers from Prison*,[5] showed that they were wrestling with questions which went to the root of the faith in which they had grown up and which had stamped the nature of their church allegiance. We have to learn to live with a God who no longer reigns above the world (as Robinson put it) or who is 'absent' and leaves the world to us human beings (Bonhoeffer). In the Roman Catholic Church, a development began with the Second Vatican Council which deeply affected the traditional pattern of worship and church life in a similar way. It was as though many people could no longer feel at home in the old and familiar patterns and were in search of more authentic and deeper religious experiences. I myself grew up in a liberal Protestant environment, and after the end of the Second World War, when I was in my early twenties, played an active role in it. The end of the Liberal Protestant Broadcasting Service (VPRO) as an expression of this milieu was characteristic of a process which took place among liberal Protestant groups and was tangible in the personal life of many of them – for some more clearly than for others. For many people the familiar liberal Protestant pattern of life lost not only its external vitality and persuasiveness but above all also its inner conviction, and as a result they were deprived of (some also felt that they had been freed from) a framework within which they had hitherto felt at home. What had hitherto been the foundation of their life, and one that they had taken for granted, faded, and they were thrown back on themselves. This is a process which has been evident not only among liberal Protestants but also among many Roman Catholics, orthodox Protestants and even humanists. It is not clear what factors have played a role here, but as far as I can see one factor is loss of faith in the 'power' of the fathers in whose shadow we had grown up. We must now travel by our own compasses. What happened in these years – of ferment and renewal - is an answer to this challenge.

One important factor in my personal life was becoming involved with clinical pastoral training. This training, which developed in America, helps the theologian with an academic education to become a pastor by stages and under supervision; it brings him or her into contact with a learning process which appeals to a readiness to learn from mistakes and as a result to enter into a conversation with himself or herself. So this helped me not only not to avoid doubt and above all self-questioning, but also to accept it in a positive way, and as a result to become as honest and authentic as possible.

During this period I also investigated psycho-analysis more deeply and felt it necessary to take account of its verdict on religion. I wrote *Psychology of Religion*,[6] a book in which I discussed the various analytical theories of religion and in connection with this developed my own theory based on psychoanalysis. As its original Dutch title indicated, this book circled round the mystery of religion, and as a result it became much clearer to me how to reflect on that mystery. What is the mystery of religion? Does it have an impregnable nucleus, a demonstrable nature which can be defended? What are our religious experiences about?

In the winter of 1980-1981 I was visiting professor at Princeton Theological Seminary in the United States; there I met James Loder, who had just written a book entitled *The Transforming Moment*, which made a contribution to what he described in the subtitle as 'an understanding of convictional experiences', in other

4

words to a theory of religious experience.[7] It was an attractive and scholarly book which, starting from a decisive experience in the author's own life, gave a broad and at the same time deep analysis of the structure and the content of religious experience as a phenomenon in the life of the human soul. I wrote a long review of the book, comparing it with a European book on a similar theme (a study entitled *Mit Symbolen Leben*, 'Living with Symbols', by Joachim Scharfenberg and Horst Kämpfer)[8] – and in so doing tried to gain more insight into religious experience.[9]

The result was to bring out a marked contrast. The American author, James Loder, argued that religious experience comes into being as a result of an experience of what he calls a void, an emptiness, an abyss on the one hand, and encounter with Christ on the other. For him the story of Christ's meeting with the disciples near Emmaus related in Luke 24.13-15 is a clear example of this.

The stress that the author puts on the experience of the void seems to me to be typically American: as I showed in my article, in the depths of American society there is anxiety about chaos, about a void. By contrast, the other book, by Scharfenberg and Kämpfer, had a markedly European stamp. Its starting point was the view that in our modern society we are confronted with an erosion of the significance of symbols. Many symbols which have occupied a central place in religious life down the centuries seem to be losing their power. The authors of this book see it as the task of the churches to revive these symbols. The book draws our attention to the problem of the secularization of European (and American) society. The old symbols stil exist, but they are in danger of fading away. How can we turn this process in another direction? But there is no mention of Loder's void here.

But there are points of agreement between the two books. Essential to both is that what is at issue is an experience of presence. A divine presence is disclosed in Christ and in the symbol. I have taken this word 'disclose' from the English theologian Ian T. Ransey, who in an attractive study entitled *Models and Mystery* showed how religious experience consists in the disclosure of a mystery which we can denote (he uses the word qualify) but which is always inexhaustible (here he uses the word 'elusive').[10] For Loder, the presence of Christ abolishes the void, the sense of standing before an abyss, and for Scharfenberg and Kämpfer the divine presence revives the symbol.

Behind the theme of the experience of presence, therefore, we can detect the problem of the place of religion and church in our modern society. Secularization attacks religious experience and thus the life of the church. A particular form of unbelief overgrows faith. Can it be that a study of religious experience as the experience of presence can help us to more insight into the problems of secularization?

An American book

This question pressed in on me increasingly clearly and so it was understandable that my attention should have been attracted by a review in an American journal of a book entitled *The Elusive Presence*, by Samuel Terrien, Emeritus Professor of Old Testament at Union Theological Seminary, New York.[11] I wondered whether one could say that the Bible was concerned with an 'elusive presence' and whether this could shed light on the problems of religious experience today.

Biblical theology can be defined as systematic reflection on the message of the Old and New Testaments. Biblical theologians are looking for the ideas which hold the Bible together. One can see the Bible as a collection of often divergent testimonies of faith and then ask what it is that these witnesses have in common. What binds them together? Or, to put it in more specific terms, in the Old and New Testaments we are confronted with different kinds of literature: all kinds of statements about God, about his relationship to human beings, in stories, in songs, in letters, in philosophical arguments, and also in all kinds of liturgical patterns and regulations and finally in a variety of moral commandments. The question to which biblical theology tries to give an answer is: how do we find the connecting link in all this? In what does the unity consist?

For a long time there has been a famous answer to this question.

We find it, for example, in the classical biblical theologies of Eichrodt and von Rad.[12] But it is even older than that. Our Calvinist ancestors already formulated it when they spoke of the Bible as the books of the Old and New Covenant. According to this answer the relationship of God to humankind is characterized by the concluding of a covenant. However, Terrien's book questions this. He recognizes that the covenant plays an important role in the Bible, but he does not think it possible to say that the covenant is the central theme. First of all he notes that the Old Testament speaks of two covenants which conflict with one another, the covenant made on Sinai and the later covenant with David. Secondly, he argues that the idea of the covenant is absent from large parts of the Old Testament: from certain of the prophets and the so-called wisdom literature. It also occurs only sporadically in the New Testament. Terrien argues that the idea of the covenant is secondary to the experience of God's presence. The rites and ideology of the covenant are, he says, dependent on that.

Terrien's book is therefore built up on the idea that what he calls a 'unique theology of presence' is central to both the Old Testament and the New. And he uses the word unique, first because this theology occupies a quite distinctive place amongst the religions of the Near East, and secondly because it has its roots in a unique 'elusive presence' of God. So we cannot understand the religion of Israel and the religion of the first Christians which emerged from it unless we see that its heart is this unique experience of the 'elusive presence' of God.

This position is substantiated in the book, at length and with many arguments. Terrien discusses in succession the appearances to the patriarchs and that on Sinai; he talks about the presence of God in the temple, the visions of the prophets, the singing about God in the Psalms, and the way in which God is spoken of in Job and Ecclesiastes; finally he discusses the belief in the coming of God in the last days. He deals with the New Testament much more briefly: this is about God's presence in Jesus Christ and in the first communities; my impression is that a more extensive treatment would also have brought to light more of God's 'elusive presence' in the New Testament as well.

Some texts

To demonstrate the direction of Terrien's thinking, I want to discuss briefly a few texts that he deals with. The first is Exodus 33.18-23. There we read about a conversation between Yahweh and Moses:

> Moses said, 'I pray thee, show me thy glory.' And he said, 'I will make all my goodness pass before you, and will proclaim before you my name "The Lord" and I will be gracious to whom I will be gracious, and will show mercy on whom I will show mercy. But,' he said, 'you cannot see my face; for you shall not see me and live.' And the Lord said, 'Behold, there is a place by me where you shall stand upon the rock; and while my glory passes by I will put you in a cleft of the rock, and I will cover you with my hand until I have passed by; then I will take away my hand, and you shall see my back; but my face shall not be seen.'

When we remember that these texts had their original setting in the existence of believers, because they were regularly read aloud in the liturgy, as Terrien keeps telling us, we can understand how such stories on the one hand convey human ideas about God while on the other hand simultaneously demonstrating a theological concern. For Moses, i.e. for a human being, while God is present in this story he cannot be seen: his glory remains invisible. He can, however, be heard: his name is proclaimed. The presence of God is thus indicated in this story in a particular way: God is 'elusive', he withdraws himself, he can only be heard and cannot be seen. For Terrien this contrast between audibility and visibility is an essential part of religious experience: in his book he talks of the clash between theologoumena (unfortunately he does not explain precisely what he means by this word in connection with his view of the experience of God) of the ear and the eye, the name and the glory. So religious experience as the Bible speaks of it is an experience of God's presence which comes to us through hearing, and this experience is in tension with a will to be seen which is not matched by a capacity for seeing on the human side.

The second text that I have chosen is I Kings 8.27-30. This is part of the prayer which Solomon utters at the inauguration of the temple:

> But will God indeed dwell on the earth? Behold, heaven and the highest heaven cannot contain thee; how much less this house which I have built! Yet have regard to the prayer of thy servant and to his supplication, O Lord my God, hearkening to the cry and to the prayer which thy servant prays before thee this day; that thy eyes may be open night and day toward this house, the place of which thou hast said, 'My name shall be there,' that thou mayest hearken to the prayer which thy servant offers toward this place. And hearken thou to the supplication of thy servant and of thy people Israel, when they pray toward this place; yea, hear thou in heaven thy dwelling place; and when thou hearest, forgive.

In the Old Testament we find a striking ambivalence over the temple in Jerusalem. David is not allowed to build it and the prophets often criticize it, but at the same time it is the place where God dwells: one thinks of the rites on the great Day of Atonement and of many of the psalms. This prayer of Solomon clearly expresses a compromise. Not God himself, but his name will be there: so the house itself is not divine. In other words, God remains the invisible one.

The third text is Isaiah 6.1-13, the well-known vision in which Isaiah receives his call:

> In the year that King Uzziah died I saw the Lord sitting upon a throne, high and lifted up, and his train filled the temple. Above him stood the seraphim; each had six wings: with two he covered his face, and with two he covered his feet, and with two he flew. And one called to the other and said:
> 'Holy, holy, holy is the Lord of hosts;
> the whole earth is full of his glory.'

And the foundations of the thresholds shook at the voice of him who called, and the house was filled with smoke. And I said: 'Woe is me! For I am lost; for I am a man of unclean lips, and I dwell in the midst of a people of unclean lips; for my eyes have seen the King, the Lord of hosts!'

Then flew one of the seraphim to me, having in his hand a burning coal which he had taken with tongs from the altar. And he touched my mouth, and said: 'Behold, this has touched your lips: your guilt is taken away, and your sin forgiven.' And I heard the voice of the Lord saying, 'Whom shall I send, and who will go for us?' Then I said, 'Here I am! Send me.' And he said, 'Go, and say to this people:
"Hear and hear, but do not understand;
see and see, but do not perceive."
Make the heart of this people hard,
and their ears heavy,
and shut their eyes;
lest they see with their eyes,
and hear with their ears,
and understand with their hearts,
and turn and be healed.'
Then I said, 'How long, O Lord?'
And he said:
'Until cities lie waste without inhabitant,
and houses without men,
and the land is utterly desolate,
and the Lord removes men far away,
and the forsaken places are many
in the midst of the land.
And though a tenth remain in it,
it will be burned again,
like a terebinth or an oak,
whose stump remains standing when it is felled.'
The holy seed is its stump.

The striking thing about this passage is that there is more openness here towards seeing God, but at the same time there is mention of a transcending of human vision. And there is certainly no mention of 'enjoying' glory. Human beings do not participate in any way in the divine vision. On the contrary, in this passage too the emphasis is on hearing, on the word of command.

Psalm 27.4-7 carries further the line which we could see in Isaiah:

One thing have I asked of the Lord
that I will seek after,
that I may dwell in the house of the Lord
all the days of my life:
to behold the beauty of the Lord,
and to inquire in his temple.
For he will hide me in his shelter in the day of trouble;
he will conceal me under the cover of his tent,
he will set me high upon a rock.
And now my head shall be lifted up above my enemies round
about me;
and I will offer in his tent sacrifices with shouts of joy;
I will sing and make melody to the Lord.

Here we can see that the ambivalence over the temple has disappeared: the beauty of God is present there and one may look on it. The line of seeing is clearly present and there is no mention of the ear or of hearing. Remarkably enough, Terrien goes on to speak of the motherly side of God on the basis of this psalm. In my view we can perhaps even say that there is a degree of participation in God: 'Do not abandon me', the psalmist prays in v.9.

This is only a brief selection from the wealth of Old Testament texts with which Terrien deals. However, I hope that it gives an impression of the way in which he sees the problems connected with God's presence in the Old Testament. In his discussion of the New Testament Terrien again chooses a number of texts in which we can see the two lines of name and word on the one side and glory on the other. He sees the three main elements of the Christ event – the annunciation, the transfiguration and the

11

resurrection – as an 'original interpretation of the Hebrew theology of presence' along the line of the word, and the idea of the community as the (new) temple of the spirit as an interpretation along the line of the visible glory. However, one can bring his view of these problems even closer to the experience of believers and argue that the line of the word and the ear appears above all in the Synoptic Gospels: there Jesus makes God present in his words (and actions), whereas he himself is constantly 'elusive'. One thinks of the discussion of the Messianic secret in his life. Over against this stands the Gospel of John as the Gospel in which the line of the eye, of becoming visible and of participation, becomes tangible: in John 1.14, for example, we read that 'The word was made flesh and dwelt among us and we have seen his glory.' This is also the Gospel in which there is constant emphasis on community and on love. In the images in which Jesus speaks of himself here – the shepherd, the vine, the bread, the water – we find the same thing. In my view, Paul in his letters is closer to the line taken by the Synoptic Gospels.

A unique experience

So what Terrien argues is that there is a specific biblical experience of God and also a spirituality based on the Bible, though in it we are confronted with the problem of two divergent lines, which stand in a kind of relationship of tension to each other. In this spirituality I see the summit of the mountain which we are to climb on our journey in this book. Through Terrien's book we get as it were a view of this summit. So I want first to examine Terrien's book rather more closely. There are a number of things in it which concern us – if we let it speak to us.

In the first place, Terrien constantly stresses the uniqueness of the biblical experience of God. This is evidently true against the background of the nature religions of the Near East, amongst which the Old Testament has a distinctive stamp of its own – one thinks of the Canaanite gods and their cult. However, the question arises: is that also true of Islam? Is there not also, as I have argued elsewhere, a clear parallel between the faith of Israel and Islam?[13]

In Islam as in Israel we see an anti-mystical trait, an opposition to the veneration of images and a stress on the significance of the word. This agreement leads to the questions which I discussed in detail in my *Psychology of Religion*, whether a particular pattern of culture or upbringing does not have a role here, and especially whether in these two cases the relationship of children to the father in the family is not a decisive factor.[14] This is a point to which we shall certainly have to return later.

Secondly, Terrien's book raises the question whether in his biblical theological reflections we do not have more psychology than theology. Is the uniqueness of which he speaks not above all a specific experience of God's elusive presence and does not the exposition and analysis of this experience make his argument psychological rather than theological in character? One of the attractive aspects of the book is that it is written in so warm a way, is so inspiring by nature and so uplifting in its tone. Is not this the case because it is about human experiences and not about theological positions and certainly not about theological speculations?

However, this means that at some points it is theologically vulnerable, for example in what it says about the covenant. We have already seen that the idea of the covenant has a central place in biblical theology. Terrien wants to contrast with this the idea of God's 'elusive presence'. In my view he is mistaken here. In theology we reflect on the content of faith and talk about that in which we believe. That is rather different from speaking about what we experience. We cannot experience a covenant between God and humankind. We can conclude a covenant and (or) believe in it, that it has been concluded and that we may therefore trust in it. However, we can experience God's presence.

There is a connection between the experience of the presence of God and belief in a covenant between God and humankind. We see this connection in the case of Moses. But *how* are these two connected? Terrien argues that the experience is primary and the covenant is secondary, but in the two passages in which he goes into this relationship more deeply he shows that there is an organic connection. This remains a weakness of his book.

13

However, for me the important contribution of his study is to show that presence is an essential characteristic of religious experience, even in Israel.

Thirdly, Terrien argues that this presence is 'elusive', but he does not give a clear definition of what for him is an essential concept. So first we must look at that more closely. It is a particularly important concept specifically in connection with spirituality.

For Terrien, 'elusive' means that the presence of God is a presence in absence. This elusive presence is especially characteristic of the religious experience in both Old and New Testaments. As we can see in all kinds of stories – one might think of the appearances to Moses at the burning bush or on Sinai, of those to the prophets like Elijah, or of the words of Solomon at the dedication of the temple – it means that God is never visible, but can be heard. It is clearly part of religious experience that human beings have a need to feel and to know that God is near, but within the religious pattern of the Bible this need is never fully satisfied. God is 'elusive', as Terrien says; in other words he is far too exalted for people to be able to know that he is so near. There remains a certain distance, indeed a gulf, between God and humanity. Terrien keeps arguing that there is no mention in biblical piety of mysticism, of a fusion or a merger. All the stress is on the word. God himself is unattainable, transcendent. In the same way Karl Barth speaks of the *finitum non capax infiniti* (the finite cannot comprehend the infinite) and of the 'line of death' which separates God from humankind and human beings from one another. Therefore for Terrien the word 'faith' is characteristic of biblical piety; it includes an answer to a word and therefore above all implies obedience.

Here Terrien puts great stress on the significance of the liturgy. The liturgy is the setting for the Old Testament text, in other words for the narratives, the psalms, the prophetic books and even the book of Job. This liturgy is in origin a repetition of the stories in order to keep alive the relationship to God's presence, even when this is no longer experienced directly. Thus in biblical piety in the strict sense there are no holy places or images through which one can experience God's presence. What Terrien calls 'liturgical trust' maintains the relationship with God.

In all this we must remember that in Israel a degree of tension comes into being over against the Near Eastern environment, and especially over against the other type of religion that is present in it. This is a religion with images, with chthonic rites and festivals, even with temple prostitution. Marriages resulted in something like a mixture, or at least a confrontation, between the two types. The kings in Jerusalem were the embodiment of this, and evidently it provoked all kinds of reactions among the people. According to Terrien, in the North people were Yahwistic in an old-fashioned way, whereas in the south and especially in Jerusalem the population was more open to other influences. I would add here that we must also note a tension within Yahwism itself. The transcendence of God with its elusive character evoked among some believers, perhaps among all, a need for nearness and experience. I argued in my *Psychology of Religion* that in this way we can see a need for mysticism in Islam, comparable with the need for a certain 'piety' in Calvinism.[15] Terrien refers to the existence of two types of theology in Yahwism. I would prefer to speak of two types of piety, or possibly spirituality. We have already seen how a theology of the name is different from a theology of glory. The first is the earliest; it is prophetic and sees life as a pilgrimage. The second feels an affinity to the temple, the land and the royal dynasty: this last makes possible a syncretistic fusion with Near Eastern religions, customs and ideas. It experiences life more as a matter of being taken up into a holy order. I think that Barth would call this second type 'religion' and see it as a contrast to typically biblical faith. If my view is correct, we have a parallel to this second type in our earlier 'Christian' view of society, in 'Christendom': the association of God and nation in a holy order, the combination of throne and altar. For Barth, this view too fell under the heading of 'religion'.

15

'Elusive presence'

Against this background, the word elusive calls for closer reflection. We must ask ourselves whether it is adequate to express what Terrien indicates as being the essential characteristic of the biblical experience of God. In fact Terrien's argument is really about two types of religion. In the first type God is experienced above all as being transcendent, and thus as elusive. He does not show himself, but only makes himself heard. His medium of revelation is the name, the word. In the second type God becomes visible and even tangible in holy objects and holy people. His medium of revelation is the image, which gives a reflection of his glory. But here too his presence is not always immediately at human disposal. People have to prepare themselves, 'purify' themselves, in order to be admitted to his presence. So here too human beings experience godforsakenness, standing before the void, the void of being left alone. Here too God is elusive in a particular, but different way. One must undergo a course of purification, of detachment, of meditation, in order to find him.

Thus two different ways of experiencing God go with these two types of religion and two types of spirituality with them. We shall have to return to this in more detail.

Before we do that, I want to look at the question of the effect of the presence of God in human life, in other words the question of the significance of a relationship with God for men and women. In his book Terrien does not go explicitly into this question, but implicitly he gives a picture of his view of the problem.

According to Terrien's accounts the presence of God in the texts of the Old Testament has three aspects. In the first place it is related to the people. The presence (i.e. God) wills to be there for the people. What prophets like Elijah or Isaiah experience are not primarily individual experiences – they are only secondarily that – but they contain a message, a commission, for the people; the presence of God in their (individual) experience is thus directed through them to the people. The same is true of Moses and the writers of the Psalms. Only in Job and Ecclesiastes do we find an experience with a more personal focus, but even here it does not go outside the people and the relationship of the people to God.

In the second place, God's making himself present has a particular effect, indeed a purpose, namely the salvation of the people. God makes himself heard and in so doing makes his presence experienced in Egypt, in the wilderness, in the wars, in the exile, and in this way he delivers the people from annihilation, from death, from what Terrien sometimes calls cosmic solitude. In other words, in its confrontation with nothingness, with death, with the void, the people experiences the presence of its God as the last and decisive salvation. In the life of us men and women God's presence is related to nothingness.

Thirdly, the presence of God also has a particular effect on the people. It produces a degree of coherence. It so to speak welds the people together so that they have a feeling of unity and consequently of communal obligation. It is rather like the relationship of a king with his people. Here we find the same thing, so it is no coincidence that God is called the king of the people. Indeed we can go a step further: a people finds its identity in relationship to its ruler. The Jewish people exists as a people through its relationship with its God-king. Without him it falls apart; then it is divided, weak, and perishes in strife and chaos. We can also think of a family: without parents the children have no name and thus no identity. When the parents are not at home they begin to squabble.

What I have said so far should have made clear the main outlines of the book. Reverting to the picture of the mountain climb I would want to say that in this book we get a view of the summit of the mountain that we want to climb. In so doing we keep in mind that we are concerned with our spirituality, with a life with and through our relationship to the mystery of God in our existence. What strikes us now in this book? What seems important to us in it?

Those who allow the book to speak will note that it ends up in a tension which is present in religious experience. Human beings are aware of the elusiveness of God and try to hold fast to his presence. Terrien shows that here two lines are visible in the Old

Testament. On the first line there is an attempt to hold fast to God by telling stories about appearances that God has made: this is a fixed ritual in the liturgy. The liturgy takes place in sanctuaries, above all in the north of the country: Shechem is one of the centres. Along the second line there is an attempt to make God present: this takes place in the temple through specific liturgical actions like sacrifices. Here Jerusalem is the great centre and the prime focus is with priesthood and kingship. Along this line concessions are often made to paganism, usually for the sake of the foreign wives of the kings, but in my view the problem is posed too simply if one fails to see, as I have just shown, that along this line an attempt is also made at a solution of an internal problem of Yahwism itself.

Of course on closer inspection one can see all kinds of religious phenomena in the Old Testament – and also in Islam – which can also be regarded as attempts to slacken the tension caused by the transcendent experience of God. I have already referred to the development of mysticism. But can one not also regard the observance of the Torah (there is a remarkable article by Levinas in which he shows that one must prefer the Torah to God),[16] the sabbath, circumcision, and pilgrimages from this perspective?

Two lines

So we see that the two lines are basic to our view of what spirituality is. They can be seen at all the important areas of our relationship with God. One point that is not developed by Terrien is the emergence of two types of cult and liturgy. There is a type of cult in which the word is central, in which stories are told, the scriptures are expounded, the Torah is meditated on, a type which lives on down to the present day in the synagogue and in Protestant worship. This is a type of worship in which the participants are above all asked for the reaction of their faith. And there is the type in which the divine presence is central, in which all the emphasis is on the sacrament, the sacrifice, the altar, the priest. This is the type which is visible, via the temple in Jerusalem, in Roman Catholic worship. Here a major role is played in the liturgy, not only by sacred actions, but by hymns and praise, by participation in the celebration.

Of course, the most important thing for spirituality is that in all this two types of religious experience, of the experience of God's presence, are involved. We need to look at this more closely. For the first type, God is the distant authority. He is transcendent: he can be heard, but in principle he is invisible. It is impossible to represent him in pictures and it is forbidden to make images of him and to worship them. Contact with him is through the word. His name is important. In it he reveals himself, although the name is at the same time hidden and inexpressible, a feature which indicates the elusive character of his presence. His 'revelation' is bound up with the history of his people and of the world. The aspect that dominates in the picture of God is his freedom. He is experienced as a God who intervenes: he gives laws and makes a covenant; he is critical and judges. A call constantly goes forth from him: the medium of his revelation is the ear.

In the second type God is the one who is present in the temple. Those who believe in him talk of a real presence. His revelation is bound up with a sacral priesthood, with a particular cult, with a holy mountain and a holy city. Here the stress does not fall on his name but on his glory: the medium of his revelation is the eye.

I have already pointed out that the New Testament also shows these two lines. For example we can say that in terms of the type of spirituality that I have described, Paul and John are opposites, and that the Synoptic Gospels must be put on the same side as Paul. In Paul we clearly find the prophetic type: as Paul says, faith comes from hearing; for him the call, the word, stands first. God is experienced above all as the God of the covenant and the law (Paul does not deny his Pharisaic upbringing here). As with the prophets, God reveals himself near Damascus as the God who is involved, whereas for Paul Jesus is above all the Messiah, the one who is sent, whom people must follow and obey and with whom he has no mystical relationship. In John, as we saw, already in the prologue the emphasis is on seeing the glory of Christ, and being involved in the community plays a major role throughout the Gospel.[17] The prophetic stress on the word is less strong; there is less indication that the apostle is the one who is sent out. In the farewell discourses one can recognize the seeing of glory and thus a certain kind of mystical relationship to Christ, in which belonging to him plays a major role.

We can similarly discover both lines in church history. Among Catholics of different types we find a predilection for the Gospel of John, and the emphasis on glory that is bound up with that: emphasis on the unity of the community, images, the role of the eye, mysticism and finally an openness to natural theology, coupled with a degree of syncretism. In the Reformed tradition the influence of Paul is much stronger, the emphasis on the word predominates and the gulf between God and humankind is of fundamental significance. An anti-syncretistic tendency is also evident: one thinks of Barth's criticism of religion.

One can go even further and note how both lines can also be seen in other areas of church life and religious life. Here I am thinking of church buildings. There are churches which are characterized by a deliberate emptiness: some mosques, certain Reformed church buildings, places where the word is central. And there are cultic buildings where open yet filled spaces form another holy reality, places where the divine is present. Roman Catholic churches are of this type: they can give one the sense of being taken up into a 'presence' which is perhaps not present in the strict sense of the word, but is clearly represented. Gothic churches can evoke the feeling of an elusive presence that is there in the second line, that of glory.

Two types of worship go with these two types of church building. First of all there is the type in which the emphasis falls on listening, on reflecting, on deciding, and in which all the rites take place on this level. We might think of the celebration of the sabbath in the synagogue, in which everything is focussed on the singing and on reflection on the Torah, or of a Protestant service, in which the liturgy finds its focal point in the reading and exposition of a fragment of the text of the Bible. But alongside that there is the type of participation, in the eucharist, in which the rites are performed on the level of this participation, physically in kneeling, moving, following with the eyes, and above all also spiritually in preparation and meditation. Listening to a sermon is merely one part of this liturgy.

In both types of worship the aim is also different. In the first type the concern is to recall, to become involved again, to learn, through the stories which are listened to and expounded. The singing of hymns is an emotional reaction to this recalling, a retelling and stressing of what is heard. In the second type the aim is to make it present again and provide an occasion for participation in it. The hymns that are sung here are an attempt to intensify this participation emotionally.

It seems clear to me that what I have described here are ideal types. In practice, in personal and church life, we can see all kinds of mixed forms – even in Israel. The important thing seems to me to be that we have seen that there is a polarity in the colourful palette of biblical spirituality and that this polarity has in turn coloured religious, church life down the ages. This polarity is set against the background of the fundamental experience of the void, the abyss, with which people are confronted, and of the saving presence of God over against it. The essential element in this experience is, however, at the same time that the presence is elusive and that it therefore eludes human grasp. God remains the great absent one in his presence. However, in human experience this absence is disclosed in two ways, that of the name and that of the glory. The distant God can be near to us in his word and in the sacrament, the temple, the sanctuary. If we want to talk about spirituality, we cannot avoid this polarity.

Some questions

Finally, a brief look at some questions which will doubtless have occurred to us. First of all: do we recognize all this in our own life and is it therefore more than just a bit of biblical theology which arouses the curiosity of us men and women of the twentieth century? Secondly, can we say anything to explain the problems of this spirituality? And thirdly, can we rise above this polarity?

First of all, do we recognize ourselves in it? I suppose that some things will not be alien to us. We are confronted with a void when

21

we are thrown back on ourselves through death and suffering. That is true for people both inside and outside monasteries. But we also recognize that we can respond to this with acceptance, following one of the two lines indicated by Terrien, that of faith in the word, in the name, and through the stories which we tell one another at liturgical gatherings. Or we can respond to it along the other line through finding a basis for living by participating in the sacrament, by participating in God's presence in his glory. We also recognize ourselves in the stress on the significance of the presence of God not only for men and women as individuals but also for the world as a whole, for people generally. And in all this we also know the temptations, the arbitrariness, the doubt, the lack of love, the obscurity of existence, in short all the things that darken human life in the Bible.

The second question is whether we can find a psychological explanation for these two lines in religious experience. In my book *Psychology of Religion* I defended the hypothesis that the differences in types of religion are connected with differences in patterns of relationship, especially in the patterns of relationship of parents and children.[18] There are maternal and paternal types of religion. What I want to argue in the present book develops this hypothesis.

Some Belgian researchers have studied the images of God that men and women have. It emerges that relationships with parents play a decisive part here. In a variety of publications Anton Vergote in particular has shown that images of God contain two elements, first of all a maternal one, which he describes as availability, and secondly a paternal one, which is characterized by law and authority.[19] The affinity of these two elements with Terrien's two lines is unmistakable: participation in presence presupposes availability, and faith in the sense of obedience and trust is an extension of law and authority. We shall investigate this hypothesis more fully later in this book.

The third question is: can we transcend this polarity? If we let Terrien's book speak to us and investigate the results of discussions in the ecumenical movement so far we must conclude – at least provisionally – that it is difficult to see the polarity being transcended within theology. We are opposed to one another on fundamental points, and see little chance of achieving any consensus on marginal issues – like discussions over ministry.

Is it conceivable that non-theological factors also play a part here and that as a result of a study of these factors we can come to a greater understanding of one another's standpoints, so that a more satisfying conversation and thus deeper ecumenical contact becomes possible? Some work has already been done in this sphere, and it is becoming clear that for example social patterns in the area of religious and church life play a greater role than people often suppose. I personally believe – and I hope that I shall demonstrate this in the present book – that urban, technological society in particular has a profound influence on religion and church, and that we have not studied this anything like enough. In addition I am convinced that we shall be able to make important discoveries from psycho-analysis with its investigation of parent-child relationships. I also hope to be able to demonstrate that in this book. However, we are still only at the beginning of a development and therefore at present it is hard to say how far sociological investigations can contribute to the construction of a better theology. Perhaps some prospects will emerge through my hypotheses.

Through Terrien's book, in this chapter we have been able to catch a glimpse of the summit towards which our journey will take us. Now we must begin at the foot.

two

At the Foot

In the previous chapter we were concerned with the question of God's presence in the Old Testament and the New Testament. The question was: what religious experience is present there? What is the structure of this experience and what spirituality is connected with it? We assumed that the roots of this religious experience are to be found deep in human development. That is the point at which I want to begin our reflections in this chapter.

I suggest that we begin from the idea that our journey starts in a Swiss mountain village. Think of Zermatt, from which the top of the Matterhorn can be seen so impressively in the distance. It is still early in the morning, only half light, and rather misty. The outlines of the houses are blurred. In the distance we hear human voices; that gives us a feeling of confidence. We are not alone. But these voices are also blurred, impossible to make out. So are we alone? We live in a sphere of expectation. Soon the day will break, but we have to wait. That is the starting point for our mountain climb.

This chapter is concerned with our childhood years, the years in which we live in our family and in its immediate environment. These are years of which we have only vague recollections; we have almost complete amnesia (loss of memory) for the very first years. But a good deal happened in these years. There were many things and people around us, and we sensed it all vaguely: we found it difficult to get a grip on them. There were people, our parents, who gave us the feeling that we could have confidence in life, that we were not alone; and at the same time we had the feeling, though in contact with them, that we were alone. They were sometimes away and we had to learn to be alone. There was also an atmosphere of expectancy in these childhood years. Sometimes new things happened to us, we became curious; we found everything that we experienced and were to be very important. But it was always a time when we had to wait; we remained dependent.

What do we really know about these first years of life? I have to begin with some theory. We know various things about these first years of our life from psycho-analysis. In the first place we know it through the interpretation of dreams and in the second place through phenomena that we perceive in what is called transference in the contact between the psychotherapist and the patient, in the feelings which each has to the other.[1] These dreams and these behavioural phenomena in transference are interpreted in psycho-analysis, and as a result of this we can arrive at some kind of knowledge about the very first experiences and feelings in the life of a child. The second thing that we can know about these first years is based on a certain number of observations that we can make of children. René Spitz wrote a well-known book about the first year of a child's life, in which he observed the child's behaviour from the first day of its life and also interpreted various patterns with the help of psycho-analysis.[2] It is important for us to remember that psycho-analysis itself has undergone some development. It began with the interpretation and perception of certain phenomena in the later years of a child's life and from there progressed in its investigation to the earlier years; this was as it were a progress from above downwards.

As far as the role of the parent was concerned, psycho-analysis at first stopped at the role of the father and only later went on to that of the mother. For example, for Freud the role of the father is almost central in the life of the child. For him the Oedipus complex is the most important complex in the child's development.[3] After that, increasing attention was paid to the role of the mother in psycho-analysis.[4] Here one might think of English psycho-analysts, researchers like Klein and Bowlby, who have investigated the reactions of the child to being abandoned by its mother.

Heinz Kohut, one of the most recent researchers and theoreticians in the sphere of psycho-analysis, takes us a step further. He offers a new approach. He comments that before the developments which Freud and the English analysts have said to be fundamental to the life of the child, a particular development takes place which he calls the development of the self.[5] The child's self develops, he says, in contact with the mother. In my view, here there is a discovery of things which are also important for us as theologians. In short, one can say that the presence of the mother in the life of the child is a basis for the experience of the presence of God. That explains how someone like Vergote can say that there are also specific maternal features in the image of God. We need to consider this rather more closely. In general we can note that the relationship of the child to its mother and father influences its relationship to God. Vergote and his Belgian colleagues have shown that one rediscovers the images of one's parents in one's image of God. Vergote begins from the notion that Christianity is a father religion, and he shows how the idea of the law and that of authority play an important role in the image of God. But he also shows that there are clear maternal features in the image of God, for example, availability. In my view this availability is connected with the presence of God.

We may say that there is projection, but what is it, and how is it possible? Evidently there is something in our relationship with God that also exists in our relationship with our parents. We find the clearest comments about this in Freud. He says that our relationship to God is really a regression, a reversion to our relationship with our parents. In our relationship to God, our wish to continue to be protected seems to play a major role: we seem to need to to continue to be protected by our parents. However, according to Freud, this is of course an illusion.[6] His ideas have been very influential; many intellectuals of our time have the same view of religion as Freud.

I shall not go more deeply into this point at present. I believe that we can say that while this regression does occur, such a view of religion does not fit in with authentic religion. Authentic religion is much more adult, and not childish. In my account in

Psychology of Religion, I took over the concept of 'release' from animal psychology.[7] The concept of release means that in the relationship to its parents something is released in the child which can later play an independent role in its life. So one can say that as a result of a child's relationship to its father something comes into being which can be called obedience. Obedience to God, to law and to authority is therefore that which is released in the child by the father. In this way particular religious patterns come into being. I have shown in my *Psychology of Religion* that there are types of relationship to God which have a basis in particular patterns of development. We know from psycho-analysis that psychological development takes place in phases. There are three phases in the relationship between the child and its parents: the oral, the anal and the Oedipal phases. My view is that the patterns which are released in these phases have an influence on later relationships with God. I shall examine them briefly here.

First, then, there is the oral phase. In this phase the mouth has a central role, but so to does touch, being cuddled, something which is experienced by the child as participation in the mother. As a result of this participation there comes into being in the child a trust, a primal trust. However, this trust must overcome a mistrust, the other side of the feeling that the mother really cannot be trusted, because sometimes she abandons the child. A profound element in human development in the depths comes about in this polarity. Erikson says that in this polarity something comes into being that we shall later call religion.[8] He has demonstrated that in more detail in a study of the significance of rites in human life. He says that the presence of the mother is always experienced in rites, rites which we later find in the liturgy and in spirituality, in short in the sphere of religion.

After the oral phase comes the anal phase, the phase in which human beings gain some independence, in which achievement begins to play a major role and the accent falls on fashion and order, on status. As I have argued in more detail in my *Psychology of Religion*, the figure of the Pharisee comes into being in this religious pattern. What is developed here is also an aspect of later spirituality: for example scrupulosity in Roman Catholic piety and the stress on purity in later Calvinism.

The third phase is the so-called Oedipal phase, in which the stress lies on initiative and in which the son feels himself to be, or can feel himself to be, a rival to his father. This is the phase in which the father is a model for him, but at the same time is imagined as a punitive authority. The father enters the child's life in the form of the super-ego, so that one can say that the presence of the father in the life of a child is experienced as a command or as an ideal, but always in a relationship of distance: one could say in the pattern of the relationship between the king and his subject. What I want to stress here is that the pattern of relationship between parents and children can clearly influence the later relationship of men and women to God, and especially the images of God that they have later. In all this we can see two lines developing. One line is that of the experience of God on the mother's side. God is experienced as available, as Vergote puts it, as the place where one feels secure, of which one can gain a part, through which one experiences something of liberation. This is the line of mysticism and also the line of contemplation, the general line of Catholic piety.

The other line is that in which God is primarily experienced as the Father, the King, the line in which the distant authority in God is stressed. God is experienced here at a distance. There is no mystical relationship with him, and contemplation plays only a minor role. The emphasis is far more on obedience, and thus on concepts like sin and guilt. This is the line that we find predominantly in Calvinism, and especially in the dialectical theology of Karl Barth, in which law plays a major role. It is clear that there will also be mixed forms, and we also see these mixed forms emerging in history: Lutheranism, Roman·Catholic theology, Modernism all have elements from both lines.

Lines can also be drawn from this to Terrien's book and the concept of spirituality. I shall return to the latter in due course. In Terrien we rediscover the two lines I have mentioned. He says that first of all there is the presence of God through the ear. That is the prophetic line, the line in which distance predominates, in which no mysticism is present. It is the line of obedience, of the law, of the name, of the word. But in Terrien's book there is also the other line, in which presence is experienced through the eye. Here the emphasis is on glory and there is mention of participation in God. This is the line that we find in temple piety, in the Jerusalem priesthood, with a link to the nature religions around Israel. So these two lines in Terrien clearly run parallel to the two lines which I described above: to the experience on the one hand of a God who is available on the mother's side, and on the other of a God on the father's side who is experienced as king and is encountered in the word.

We shall now go on to look more closely at the problems associated with the experience of the presence of God. In Terrien the concept of presence is not analysed in greater depth. However, he clearly indicates the effect of the presence of God. This presence speaks of nothingness. It speaks of death; it speaks of suffering. It also gives an identity. The Jewish people gains its identity in the encounter with God's presence. I think that in this area psycho-analysis, and especially Kohut, can take us further. Kohut argues that there is originally a unity, a symbiosis, between mother and child. Mother and child cannot be separated from one another by a gulf. Only slowly in the child's consciousness does the mother become an object outside itself. But the presence of the mother remains necessary for the child, so that it can grow into an adult. Kohut says that the mother is a mirror for the child: through her glance, through her smile, through her pet words, she reflects the child. Kohut goes on to explain that in situations of transference, i.e. in psychotherapeutic situations, we see what really happens here in the mother-child relationship. If the psycho-analyst is away for a weekend, or perhaps goes on vacation for a longer period, the patient can get in a kind of panic. The patient clearly needs the presence of the therapist. This presence gives reassurance. A.A.A.Terruwe, the Dutch psychiatrist, is fond of speaking of the consolidation which one person can give to the life of another.[9] Kohut makes a deeper analysis of this relationship. He says that the experience of absence can lead to fragmentation, to a falling apart: this can also turn into anger and finally also to apathy, to a feeling of emptiness, of being dead. I think that we can sense this if we imagine the experience of someone waiting for the arrival of a train with a friend on it, only to find that that the friend has not come: he or she is then confronted with a void and feels a kind of panic rising.

Years ago Willy Corsari wrote a book describing what happens in someone who gets home to find a letter on the mantelpiece in which his wife tells him that she has left him. We can also feel this panic in groups. An army can panic when the general is killed or goes away. Freud has written about this in detail in one of his books.[10] We can have the same experience, as I myself have had, in a group when the group feels that it has been left in the lurch by its leader and cannot make contact with the new leader. The group feels disappointed and becomes aggressive; its members can even say that they are sorry that it is falling apart, losing its coherence. So the presence of another brings coherence, unity, and therefore happiness, a zest for living and a feeling of freedom into the life of an individual. By contrast, when the child misses its mother, her presence, there is a feeling of anxiety in the face of chaos and fragmentation. It is an anxiety about meaninglessness, emptiness, apathy, and also an anxiety about death. It is no coincidence that almost all fairy stories begin with a child being abandoned by its mother. The child has to learn to get used to the absence of its mother and even when she is away has to remain confident that she will return. When the mother returns and is there again, certain rites usually take place. In the relationship between mother and child, as Erikson has explained, rites are particularly important and, as we know, are also very significant in the growth of trust in the religious sphere. Moreover, as Kohut says, thereafter mother and child are inevitably bound together by a matrix, by a basis of empathy.

I think that in these views we can see a clear parallel to what Terrien says. We are also reminded of what Barth says about the human experience of chaos, death and nothingness.[11] He constantly associates these three.

So all this means that the parents, and especially the mother in the first years of a child's life, really fulfil the role of God in the life of the child. They disclose the deepest mystery of existence for him or her. When the child grows up, he or she can also recognize this mystery again in other people and in other places. However, the beginning is to be found in the relationship of the child with its mother. I have said that we experience the beginning of our mountain climb here in the village. And the basic experience there is that God is a saving presence in human life.

What insight do these considerations afford to spirituality? We have seen that spirituality has to do with salvation, with salvation from depth and suffering. That is a central event in the life of the Jewish people. We have also seen that spirituality has to do with the experience of the presence of God, with this elusive presence of God, the presence of God which cannot be grasped. And we have also seen that spirituality has to do with two aspects of religious experience. As a result of its elusiveness the experience of presence is on the one hand an experience of detachment, which can be bridged by the word, and here the experience of the law plays a central role. And on the other hand this experience of presence can be articulated by the idea that as human beings we participate in the presence of God, in the sacrament and thus in glory. May we not suppose that here the connection with one's parents, the relationship with one's mother on the one hand and one's father on the other hand, becomes clearly visible? The relationship between parents and children is also first of all about salvation, and secondly about a presence which is elusive and intangible; and finally we also have the two aspects, two lines, that of the relationship with the mother and that of the relationship with the father.

We find an illustration of these ideas in a book by Emmy van Overeem, *Niet in de zachte bries* (Not in the gentle breeze), which is probably largely autobiographical. It is about Tessa. Tessa is the child of an unmarried mother. The mother works hard; she has a shop, she is a Roman Catholic and lives in the Hague. As a child Tessa goes to a Catholic school, for a while works on a newspaper, but then goes into a convent at an early stage, the famous Carmel Convent in Boxmeer near 's-Hertogenbosch. She also joins this order. The Carmelites are a strict order and under their régime, after twelve years, Tessa gradually becomes too tense. She is given a year's leave, and after this year does not return to the convent. She goes to study for a year in Tilburg and after that become a journalist. She marries someone who was once in a concentration camp and does not want to have children. She lives with her husband on a farm in North Holland. Relations between them are very difficult: among other things her husband has many problems with the concentration camp syndrome and he also finds it difficult to establish relationships. However, deep down there is a deep bond between these two people.

The writer shows Tessa as someone on a search. She is in search of herself and of God and is at the same time in search of her mother and father. She suffers from the elusiveness of these figures in her life. She needs their presence in order to find herself and to find God. As a young girl her mother had casual sexual intercourse with a young man and as a result became pregnant. This young man – the father – avoided further contact. The girl was not really accepted by her parents and she took a long time to tell them of her pregnancy. She wrestled with the problem whether she should have an abortion but did not. However, when the child came she could not really accept it and welcome it; she became shut in on herself. She began to work hard in order to buy food, and had a small shop of her own. As a result, as a young child Tessa had a really lonely life. She did not receive any real warmth; her mother had no time for her and found it difficult to understand her. This generated a kind of anger in Tessa. Later she was also to dream about it; she suppressed this anger. At the age of three she really parted company with her mother. From that time the two of them lived side by side. According to Tessa's mother, her father was dead. In reality he died much later. Tessa's father was never mentioned, but she had fantasies about him. Tessa grew up as a happy child but with a great sense of duty. There were two decisive moments in her inner development. The first was at a retreat at her school when a clergyman who was giving a lecture there spoke with much feeling about God the Father. The second was when as a journalist for her newspaper Tessa visited Poland and went to a concentration camp there. This become a decisive event for her. She stopped, paralysed, on the grass: she was confronted with death and nothingness. At this time she also heard about the Carmel convent. She wanted to join the Carmelites. Perhaps through prayer she might gain a 'magical' power with which to benefit the world. That was the thinking in the world of Carmel. In the convent she found a kind of polarity in the fixed structures of monastic life, an inner tranquillity on the one hand and later on the other a degree of tension under the heavy demands which were put to her there and which she also began to make on herself. This is a polarity which we also find in Luther in his years in the monastery.[12]

Then, because the tension became too great, she was given permission to spend a year outside the monastery. And there in the world a restless period in her existence began. She went in search: really in search of the presence of God in her life. After leaving the convent at first she had a strong feeling of freedom. Then she went out to work. But underneath, all the time she was still engaged on this inner search. She had contacts with various psychotherapists: she needed help. These psychotherapists were really sorts of mother figures in her existence, who helped her slowly to free herself from the armour in which she had put herself. We find the same thing in Luther in his contacts with von Staupitz.[13] Tessa also sought contacts with men and developed a relationship with Geert, her husband. He is really a kind of father figure, but is himself very tense as a result of his experiences in a concentration camp. The consequence is that Tessa sometimes has to support him and in this relationship with him she cannot ask many questions about herself and may not expect much for herself. In this slow growth towards liberation, one might even say towards an identity of her own, there is at the same time a religious growth. We see two lines. Tessa on the one hand experiences the influence of a motherly presence of particular people in her life; that gives her a feeling of liberation, there is more authenticity in her existence, a certain sense of a dimension of depth. One might perhaps describe this as a regression, a return to the past in support of liberation, health, the ego – an idea which plays a major role in psycho-analysis.[14] At the same time – and this is the other line – she becomes detached from her mother. As a result there is a disclosure of a religious relationship, a relationship to the depth dimension in her life. But this disclosure reveals a remarkable tension: on the one hand it is a turning away from old church patterns and on the other a desire for the powerful symbols of the church and religion, in which the holy presence is experienced inwardly.

Let me quote a passage from the book. After twenty years she meets her old confessor, Jan van Son, again:

> When she looked at him as he celebrated at the altar, she knew that he was imprisoned in formulae and gestures which were no longer his own. Jan van Son celebrated an extremely living mystery: God lives and will liberate you. But he did so in rites which no longer spoke to him and her and hundreds and thousands of others. Tessa called that praying 'round a bend'. You constantly had to translate from a distant past to today. Even twenty, thirty years ago these texts and gestures had inspired and gladdened her. Now they left her cold. Now the language of the church seldom brought her into contact with the one who was so warmly present within her. Tessa was disturbed about this: she wanted to celebrate his nearness. People need worship, communication with their Creator. 'All these fossilized adornments', she said to Fr van Son. They completely obscured the symbolism. The symbolism was about life and death today, eating and being together now, but what you heard and saw came from a museum. 'Do you think that we are living in a transitional period and that in the future a new symbolism will develop or the old symbols will become comprehensible again in a purified form?' The primal images continued to speak, Jan thought, but now they were too much obscured. Since the World Wars and since Auschwitz people wanted unveiled and direct communication with the numinous. If you have lived in a concentration camp, where you have been stripped of all our dignity and good manners have gone by the board, if you have lost everything that you possessed as a

respected citizen, then you can no longer find God in a liturgical language which is too artificial, and in a meal which no longer looks like a meal. The celebration of God's presence in worship then becomes obscure. In the concentration camps people were completely thrown back on the heart of things. They were utterly dehumanized. That was primitive but also completely authentic.

We can learn some important things for our spirituality from a book like this. In the first place, that spirituality has its basis in the first experiences of a child. It is expressed in stories, in rites, in symbols of nurture and of the church, and all this can become fossilized. However, I would add that it can also continue to support a life. Secondly, we can learn from this that in our day spirituality, through inner conflicts and the struggle for a more authentic existence, can become a search for one's own identity and authenticity and as a result become a new experience of presence, a presence for which we still have no words and the power of which we hope that we shall experience in the old rites and symbols.

In a figure like Emmy van Overeem this is clearly bound up with the fact of being a woman, with the experience of suffering, with a heightened experience of God's elusiveness and his presence in the other, in her husband, in Geert and in her own helping hands.[15] So our time has a tension of its own: between elusiveness on the one hand and presence on the other. The Jews tried to resolve this tension through the temple and the Torah, and one can say that we try to resolve it in a radical theology, in social commitment and perhaps in certain charismatic groups. What Emmy van Overeem is describing is really a mountain climb. It is the journey of someone who tries to climb up from the darkness of youth, who goes through the darkness of the wood, the darkness of the inner struggle with herself, and who then gets above the treeline into the sphere of radical purification, where she begins to try to live by an inner compass. I think that this journey is related to our journey. In this chapter we have described the beginning of our journey, life in the village, the life of our youth. Now we shall enter the darkness of the wood.

three

In the Darkness of the Wood

In the previous chapter we set out on our climb from the village at the foot of the mountain. It was still misty and dark. There was a feeling of security in the village: we talked about participation, which can lead to trust. And there was also a sense of being alone: we talked about anxiety and mistrust, about expectation and waiting.

This stay in the village is as it were an image for the first years of human life. In these years too there is a half-light; there is on the one hand a feeling of security and at the same time a sense of being alone. Erikson speaks of the polarities of trust and mistrust.[1] There is also expectation. People are curious, as Harlow's monkeys are curious and want to explore the cage.[2] And in addition to the expectation there is also the knowledge that one has to wait. So there is a clear polarization in the first years of development and this continues in later life. We can say that to be adult is on the one hand to have a basis, to have some firm foundation, and on the other hand a matter of letting loose and being let loose, of being alone. During adolescence we therefore find on the one hand curiosity, a desire to get on with life, to see life, and on the other hand anxiety: What will life bring us? How shall we get on in the void of being alone? All fairy stories, I have said, are about being abandoned. We can also say that they are all about curiosity and anxiety. This is a sign that deep down in human life there is a longing for emancipation yet an anxiety which leads to an attitude of conservatism.

We can see that in a figure like Tom Thumb. Tom Thumb feels let down by his parents and goes into the wood. The wood is nothingness, the dark, with the risk of being devoured by a giant. And we can ask ourselves whether what Tom Thumb experiences is not an image of human life. It is evidently a basic human experience to feel that one is wandering in a wood, that one is living there without a clear sense of direction.

As I said, Heidegger wrote a book about 'Holzwege', about paths in the wood which come to dead ends. Deep in our collective unconscious we have the image of life as a labyrinth. We can say that what we encounter here is the sense of life expressed in existential philosophy that we meet in people like Heidegger and Sartre, and partly also in Jaspers.[3]

On our mountain climb we now leave the village of our youth and we enter life. Here we must first go through the wood.

On the hill slopes in Switzerland there is always woodland up to a height of about 5500 feet. So the beginning of our journey goes through the wood. We can also say that when we enter life we are confronted with a particular type of thought about human existence, a particular type of spirituality. Here we might think of existentialist philosophy; and in existentialist philosophy above all of Heidegger, the author of *Holzwege*. I got to know him well when I was a student in Marburg in 1927. He was a professor there and I went to his lectures for three months. He was still young and had just written his great book *Being and Time*.[4] Later he gave courses and lectures in the Netherlands on several occasions, and I again met him several times then.

Heidegger comes from a family of farmers; he grew up and later also lived in the Black Forest. As a farmer's son he never felt at home in modern technological society. One can perhaps say that a basic problem of German society is embodied in Heidegger's life. We see that problem clearly again at present in the emergence of the 'Greens' in German politics. For Heidegger, tension between his own life and life in modern society was a tension between authentic life on the one hand and what he called inauthentic life on the other. Inauthentic life is everyday life, the life of what he calls the 'they', the life of superficiality. He is in search of the depths of existence, of authentic life. In his philosophy he wants really to live, in other words, think and feel authentically. The starting point for Heidegger's thought is that to be human is to be in the world. For him, being in the world means that there is no transcendent world above this world and that human beings are human beings as we meet them here in this world, in the social groupings of this world. This is really what Sartre means when he says that existence, i.e. human existence, comes before essence, before the essential, before concern for human existence.[5] There is no world of ideas behind or in our world, as Plato and Hegel had argued, and that means from a religious perspective that as human beings we are not God's creation. In existentialist thought God is either absent or dead.[6] What we encounter here is a new perspective on life, really a new spirituality. It is a spirituality which fits our time and is therefore present in all of us. We can also say that here we come up against modern unbelief. Unbelief, or not being religious, once took the form of materialism or hedonism, being devoted to matter or to enjoyment. But in our time unbelief is increasingly becoming non-belief, an inability and sometimes also an unwillingness to believe. We can put it this way: earlier generations experienced their life as a task, as something that had a particular meaning, indeed often as a lesson which one had to learn. And that meant that from the beginning the individual was seen as being involved in a great whole. My teacher H.T.De Graaf was fond of talking about the inexhaustible whole in which an individual has to try to find his or her place.[7] There used to be a belief in a kind of sacred order, an order of Spirit, an order of God, as this was expounded in the great systems of Thomas Aquinas or Hegel.

This belief had a spirituality of its own: a spirituality in which the emphasis was placed on contemplation, on obedience, on respect and service. It was the spirituality of *ora et labora*, of prayer and work. It was in line with this that the individual did not have the right to dispose of his or her own life: life was a gift. One could not perform euthanasia or kill oneself. That was strictly forbidden. Nowadays, however, one can hear many people saying, 'We may be alive now, but we did not ask to have to live'. In a play called *Night Mother*, which has attracted much attention in the Netherlands in recent years, there are conversations between a girl who wants to commit suicide and her mother. I shall be returning to these conversations soon. What concerns us in the attitude of the daughter is that she says: 'I feel imprisoned in life, I have too many ties; I cannot be myself. But in seeking my own death I am taking responsibility for myself, realizing my own freedom.' There is no suggestion that she could be bound in her existence to a holy transcendent order extending beyond her individuality.

In *Being and Time* Martin Heidegger is a good example of this modern attitude to life. In a sense he is still very topical. Philosophy has gone on a long way since him, for example in linguistic analysis or structuralism, but it is remarkable that he keeps cropping up. Evidently his questioning is present behind these other philosophies. There is one philosopher who in modern times takes an important step further, Emmanuel Levinas.[8] I shall be discussing Levinas in more detail later.

Heidegger

The central element in Heidegger's thinking is that human beings are thrown[9] into this world, they do not know from where nor do they know how. The only thing that he seems able to say about human existence is that a person encounters himself in this world and that he then begins to live, begins to exist, begins to be there. What does 'being there', being a human, mean? In his book Heidegger explains in his compact style what that involves.

The first important thing that he says is that the heart of human life is care.[10] And he describes this care as worry: people are always worrying about things, about plans, people, their future, themselves. The second thing involved is that there are some fundamental moods in which it becomes clear how a person, this person with care, experiences life. One of these is that life is a burden.[11] Life is evidently always difficult. So – and this is the third thing that emerges – in human life there is a notable pull, a pull towards the 'they',[12] towards others. People really are terrified of the life that comes upon them with a burden of problems and a burden of feelings, and so they take refuge in everydayness.

They allow themselves to be diverted into a superficial curiosity and superficial entertainment, and often into ambiguity. Anyone who looks through the more sensational weeklies can clearly see what Heidegger means by this 'they'. For him, however, the essential thing is that the 'they' represent an escape, an escape which on the one hand gives a degree of reassurance, indeed a degree of rest, but at the same time is also alienating. In this escape we are alienated from our authentic selves, from ourselves and from one another. That gives rise, according to Heidegger, to a certain distancing[13] between people. The life that people thus lead with one another in the 'they' is a life without a foundation, poised as it were above a void. It is also characteristic of human beings that they are aware of the future, and especially that they are finite, are directed towards death.[14] This knowledge of futurity and death is really a confrontation with nothingness, a confrontation with the void, and this confrontation generates anxiety. The 'they', taking refuge in chatter and curiosity, is really an escape from this fundamental anxiety. Over against this life in the 'they', however, deep down in ourselves there is a call. It is a call to be ourselves, in other words to look death and the void in the face and to enter into anxiety. The deepest care that human beings know is thus the concern to be authentic;[15] as Kierkegaard put it, to become an individual who realizes the meaning of life. This meaning of life is 'being there', something that we can translate as becoming independent, i.e standing in the self, standing in oneself. Here we can speak of a distinctive spirituality. It is perhaps a one-sided spirituality, but it has a certain greatness: it is heroic. It reminds me of the guards who were found in the excavations at Pompeii, who had continued to keep watch when the great disaster came. They had been ordered to stand there, and there they stood. So they were found standing guard under the lava all those centuries later.

To sum up: we are people who are on 'Holzwege' in the wood. We cannot find a way through; life is a labyrinth. We are people who, as you can hear preachers say in sermons, 'fumble along the blind walls of life'. But to be a person is to be authentic. It is to be free from illusions, free from lethargy, free also from the need to escape. It is as it were to be restored to life from death.

In the play *Night Mother* that I mentioned earlier, it is striking that the daughter who wants to commit suicide first puts everything in order for her mother. Her mother need no longer have any anxieties. In the play the daughter seems to be the tranquil, loving figure who in this way is also so to speak restored from death to life. That is freedom. So in this spirituality there is no question of heaven, nor of a fiery hell. Far less is there any thought of a miraculous deliverance through which everything will be restored to order at the end of history; there is no apocalyptic. There is no belief in a resurrection, nor any conviction about a sacred order which embraces all things. Even less is there a God as creator or as father.

In the play the daughter has decided to commit suicide and tells her mother this. It is a carefully thought out decision: her life has become a burden, her marriage has gone wrong, her son is on drugs and she herself has to struggle with epileptic fits. Even her relationship to her mother has become a burden. The mother is someone who is always trying to take possession of her, who is trying to decide everything for her, who is making her unfree. And now this action that she is to perform is the act of a free decision. She feels that it is something of herself, something authentic. Moreover the remarkable thing is that in this freedom, as I have already said, she has put everything in order for her mother, so that she need have no more anxiety about the future. The girl does not seem to have any struggle of conscience over whether her action is permissible; so there is no holy order that she has to obey. All that is said is that for a human being the most important thing is to be authentic, to be free, that to be authentic is to take one's own fate upon oneself and to look that fate, that life, straight in the eye.

But that is something that the mother cannot understand. She is full of anxiety; she cannot listen well, nor can she understand the child. For her, her daughter is her possession, something that she cannot do without. In the final scene of the play, when the decision has been implemented and the mother is standing alone on the stage, her words again express this clearly: she exclaims 'But she was my child!', and everyone in the audience has the feeling that this is a superficial reaction. It is not the reaction of someone who has understood the death of another person, but more one of what Heidegger calls the 'they'.

We can regard this as a distinctive spirituality, the spirituality of our time. It is a spirituality which we always bear in ourselves as human beings, for we too are human beings of our time. For us, faith in God is no longer something obvious, but something which must be won from life. We have to find it in the labyrinth of the wood.

We can understand how someone like Karl Barth, the person who wrote all those volumes of *Church Dogmatics*, could say at a conference that he too was really an unbeliever.[16] And we can perhaps also understand something of the person who said that he often sensed more of God in the quest of these modern figures than in many of the words of believers.

Let me give a few more examples of this modern spirituality. In the first place there is Sartre, the other famous existentialist alongside Heidegger. Sartre spent the war in France, joined the Resistance and was put in prison; he says that two things are central to his view of life. First there is the conviction that life is meaningless in itself and that we human beings must give it our own meaning. He argues as follows: there is no pre-ordained plan of life, no project which is realized as it were in our life. Existence precedes essence, precedes the essential, the universals that we find in it. The second thing that is central for him is that at heart our humanity consists in being free, in our own decision. We saw in *Night Mother* how one's own decision is the supreme one. As human beings we are as it were condemned to freedom. For Sartre, moreover, there can be no God because if there were a God he would limit our freedom. So Sartre also found marriage a problem: he was never officially married to Simone de Beauvoir, his lifetime companion. That, too, is an aspect of modern spirituality: it sometimes puts very great stress on privacy, being an individual, standing apart.

The second name is that of Irwin D. Yalom, an American

psychiatrist and author of the book *Existential Psychotherapy*.[17] In this book Yalom argues that traditional psychotherapy gives help in particular psychological conflicts. These conflicts are called neuroses: the theory is that neuroses arise as a result of repression. At an early stage a person may be confronted with traumatic, wounding events which he or she cannot accept and assimilate and therefore represses. What the psychotherapist does is to help such people to become aware of these repressed thoughts and feelings and to support them in assimilating the thoughts and feelings in an adult way. Yalom says that sometimes it is possible to trace deeper questions behind these neuroses. They are often not actually mentioned in conversations, but they are touched on. He mentions four which he discusses in detail: death, freedom, isolation and meaninglessness. Some things are striking. First, that these four problems are really the great themes of existentialism, of Heidegger and Sartre. What also strikes me is that for Yalom, too, there is no place for religion. For him life has no transcendent perspective. Our whole human life is immanent; one could say that life in this world is a labyrinth, for him even more or less a prison. Another striking feature of this book is that little is said about the limiting effect of religion as that is stressed by many Europeans. Yalom's view of religion is that while it may be attractive, essentially it is an illusion. One final point to note is that for Yalom the meaning of life consists of a committed life, an authentic involvement, though he does not say anything about what is specifically to be done. Thus in this book by Yalom, too, in the background one can find a personal, one could almost say an unbelieving, spirituality.

Yalom's view is that people have to learn to live with their void, and in so doing have to achieve a degree of self-realization: this may take the form of altruism or of devotion to a cause and possibly a degree of rebellion. In this way they have to try to achieve a degree of creativity, of self-transcendence.

We also find various examples of this spirituality in the novels of Camus.[18] These are really constantly about the human confrontation with the void, with death.

Thirdly, I would refer to three modern novels which I have

discussed in more detail elsewhere: Harry Mulisch, *De Aanslag* ('The Attack'), Marga Minco, *De Val* ('The Fall), and John Le Carré, *The Little Drummer Girl*. In Mulisch's *De Anslag* the central character has to solve the riddle of the death of members of his family in the war, which he experienced. Marga Minco describes how a woman is saved in a miraculous way when Germans descend on her family; her husband and children are taken off to a concentration camp and only she survives. Why that happened remained a riddle in her life. And in *The Little Drummer Girl* John Le Carré describes the role of a young woman who has to take part in the struggle between the Israeli and the Palestinian secret services in order to lure one of the Palestinian leaders to his capture and death.[19]

I would argue that all three books are written on the basis of a confrontation with death. In this confrontation life is experienced as a labyrinth. We live imprisoned in it and are free, yet at the same time unfree. We live in isolation, and in the face of this death life becomes meaningless. However, there is a way out of this labyrinth – and this is an important thought in all three books. Clearly there is deep within us a need for what one could call a higher truth, a truth that goes further than the meaninglessness of existence. Here I recall the old conception of the labyrinth which one finds discussed in the work of the historian of religion Brede Kristensen.[20] This is a view which is evidently present in the collective unconscious of our human existence, the view, the belief that one can arrive at life through death. I want to go back to that later.

We now return to the theme of our mountain climb. We are in the wood, we have come out of the village and are now on the first stage of our journey; there we come up against the first aspect of life. At this point I want to take a specific step in my argument. I would claim that the problems that we have encountered in the wood are the primal problems of human existence. The first problems that individuals encounter in their life are death, freedom, isolation and meaninglessness, the problems which are central to Yalom's book. These are problems which therefore already play a part in our early years and will accompany us all our lives. What Kohut has discovered in the relationship between mother and child is the primal structure of human existence: by being abandoned by their mothers, men and women are thrown back on themselves and confronted with the problems of death, freedom, isolation and meaninglessness.

This point can be clarified by using Harlow's monkeys as an example. Harlow carried out what have now become famous experiments with monkeys in a cage: in these experiments he demonstrated that monkeys are curious – and the same goes for human beings. The monkeys are first with their mothers (or rather mother-substitutes) in the corner of the cage, but then they become curious. They leave these mother-substitutes and go off exploring. Then, however, they encounter something threatening in the cage, something which comes upon them, and fly back to their mothers. In the cage for a moment they were so to speak thrown back on themselves; in other words they were alone with the threat of the wood. Security with their mothers gives them new confidence: on the one hand a kind of self-confidence, on the other hand confidence in the world outside the mother. They again become curious and go back into the cage.

Do we not have to say that certain fundamental structures of human existence are evident here? In the first place these monkeys, we human beings, are curious. We have a drive to detach ourselves from our mothers. We have a need for freedom, for independence, a need to stand on our own feet. We also have a desire to extend our world, to experience more and to understand more of the world. So we have a need for knowledge and in this we have a drive to overcome our dependence, our anxiety. We try to do that by controlling the world. Fortmann spoke of a dominant attitude to life,[21] and Heidegger speaks of his difficulties over the technological control of the world.[22] We can sum all this up in the word emancipation. Curiosity leads to emancipation. Curiosity and emancipation are the beginning of becoming human.

A second fundamental structure which becomes visible here is the experience that what we cannot understand or control is a threat. The monkeys face the threat of the void, they feel abandoned, they are isolated; they experience nothingness, death. This is the structure of alienation, alienation as a counterpart of emancipation. And the third basic structure is that security is found with the mother. The presence of the mother brings liberation from anxiety and in the second place also gives a degree of independence. Basic trust comes about through the presence of the mother, the basic trust which enables the monkey to be curious, to venture into the cage again and to control reality for himself. A mother's presence also accords some freedom for others. Through a mother's presence an individual becomes free to be open to fellow human beings. Altruism is possible on the basis of, and in connection with, basic trust. We should not forget that the mother can also do the opposite and hold on to the child. So her presence can also inhibit freedom in human life. The drive towards emancipation is then a reaction against this lack of freedom. So we can conclude that existentialist thought is the spirituality of one particular pole of our humanity, namely the pole of becoming selves, of the person who is set free and as a result does not feel tied. Fundamental to this spirituality is what Heidegger expresses by saying that human beings are thrown into this world.

Here, however, we should not forget two things. In the first place, that when men and women encounter themselves in the world they always emerge from the bond with their parents. Human beings have already experienced an emotional bond before becoming themselves, and in fact they needed this bond in order to be able to live with confidence in themselves and the world. Secondly, while those who are thrown into this world meet themselves there, they also come up against others. So they do not just emerge from a tie, but also enter into new ties. These are ties which make an ethical demand on us. The stress on the ethical in relation to the other is the contribution which Levinas tries to make to the development of existentialism. For us, being human is not just associated with isolation as Kierkegaard and Heidegger understand it, but is also a polarity. Being human is to enter into the polarity of becoming a self on the one hand and of relationship to the others, to their emotional presence and ethical appeals. In this polarity, becoming a self and this relationship influence one another. This perspective sheds a new light on spirituality. In the sphere of spirituality two fundamental questions always arise: Who am I as a human being? Who are the others to me and what am I to them? To put it more specifically: as a human being I feel that I have been thrown into this world, but who supports me in the world? Who in this world is God and where is he? And along with that comes the question: how do I escape the pressures of life in this world?

We can approach spirituality in yet another way and note that three different emphases can be placed in it. The first is that life is experienced as suffering. This happens above all in Buddhism. The second is that life can be experienced as rebellion, and this happens above all in Marxism[23] and in the thought of Camus. Finally, it can be said that life is experienced as trust; this happens in Christianity. The remarkable thing is that in all these three, solidarity with the other, the other person who suffers, is essential: in Buddhism, Marxism and Christianity suffering with the other, the suffering of the other, and suffering for the other, respectively, are central.

One can almost say that there is an ecumene of sufferers in this world. At the same time, however, there is a babel of answers to the problem of suffering. Coping with this plurality in the sphere of spirituality is one of the fundamental tasks which have to be fulfilled in our modern world.

In this chapter we have gone into the wood. We have left the village, we have entered the wood at the foot of the mountain and we are now on our way to the treeline. In the next chapter we shall dwell on the question how what we have found in the wood, in other words this type of spirituality, fits into the human landscape, into that of our individual and collective history. We shall be putting the question of the origin of modern humanity and of our modern spirituality. And where are we going? If we are to answer this question there are certain maps by which we can orientate ourselves; we need to look at these maps together. Perhaps we may also discover the direction of the treeline that we want to reach, and what we shall find there. The next chapter will therefore be concerned with an overall orientation.

* *four* *

Reading the Map

In our mountain climb we started from the village, where we were concerned with various aspects of the first years of life. We then entered the wood, where we were confronted with one pole of existence, the void. We began our life in the mountain village with a view of the summit. We saw that people are aware of an elusive presence. In this way we have knowledge of God as the child does of the presence of his or her mother and father. This is always an elusive presence, a presence in which in the deepest sense we are left alone. In the wood we took this pole seriously, the aspect that life is never without the existence of a void.[1]

In this chapter we shall pause further over this pole. We begin from the idea that we can also prepare ourselves for the journey of life, that we can ready ourselves in a specific way for our stay in the wood. However, the wood has a particular place in the landscape, in the world of human existence. This world, this landscape is around us and there are maps by which we can orientate ourselves in it and identify our place in the wood. We can ask where the wood is in the landscape. Where does it begin and where does it end? What sort of wood is it? Are there ways in the wood and through the wood? Are there particular ways of getting in and other ways of leaving it?

Three kinds of map can help us here. First we have sociological maps, made by the discipline which is concerned with the historical development of society. Secondly we have psychological maps, made by the discipline that studies individual development in human existence. Thirdly we have philosophical maps, made by the discipline that reflects on life in the wood itself.

50

We can all use these three maps: each supplements the others. What we are going to do in this chapter is to look at them more closely. That will make this something of a theoretical chapter, but I hope that the journey will not seem too remote from practical life.

In this chapter we shall above all pay attention to sociology and psychology: we have already devoted some attention to philosophy, so at most I shall be filling out what has already been said. Of course we should really also look at other preparations for the journey through the wood and up the mountain; we must take account of the provisions that we carry; we must think of our equipment, our tents, our clothing and our footwear, but for the moment I shall keep these preparations in reserve.

Sociology

First we shall look at the sociological map. One could say that sociology came into being and still exists as a result of disquiet over the development of our society. Tönnies wrote his well-known book *Gemeinschaft und Gesellschaft* as early as 1887: in this book he argues that we are in the midst of a process of development. Our society is developing from a natural, organic Gemeinschaft in the direction of a modern, organized Gesellschaft. In an attractive book *The Sociological Tradition*,[2] R.Nisbet surveys modern sociological theories; what Tönnies indicated as the great problem of modern sociology is also central for him in the development of society. He says that our society is the product of two revolutions against an old order: the industrial revolution and the French revolution. To put it simply, one can argue that we are emerging from a mediaeval society characterized by a clear, sacral order, that of the church and feudalism, and are on the way to a modern society which is characterized by the development of modern industry on the one hand and a shift of political power towards government by the people on the other. This sounds somewhat abstract, but it is not very difficult to make more specific.

One might think of the Netherlands province of North Brabant.

I lived in Tilburg from 1918 to 1925 and during this time in Tilburg and Brabant I still found relics of mediaeval society. We also see something of it in pictures from Van Gogh's Brabant period. In those years Brabant was a collection of small villages. There were the beginnings of industry in some of the cities that were founded there. However, this was an industry concentrated on some rich families which together had great economic and political power. There were few intellectual reforms and the church dominated public life. It was a kind of feudal hierarchy. At this time there was still a good deal of poverty in Brabant and much ignorance. The whole of life was dominated by a faith, sometimes almost a superstition, in a sacred order.

If we compare that with present-day Brabant, we can see how the whole of society has broken open. A network of roads now criss-crosses the whole of Brabant. We see rapidly increasing prosperity, the villages changing from small communities into large conurbations, often with very pretty bungalows. A good deal of industry has come, sometimes from international businesses like Philips and Van Doorne. There are many schools; at the moment one can find every kind of school in Brabant, from lower to higher education. Whereas formerly in Brabant society was governed by particular families, now we have to say that this control has largely vanished, or at any rate is much more diffuse. The church still plays a role in Brabant society, but it is not what it used to be. The church has been shifted from the centre more to the periphery, and there are few signs of its power church in society. As for belief in a sacred order which supports everything, this order is also often discussed by a number of younger people.

So there is much progress, but there are also obvious shadow sides. The question asked by Fortmann, 'What has happened to man?',[3] is a question that arises when we think of the development of Brabant. We see how in the midst of this increased prosperity many people are confronted with a fundamental doubt. This is a doubt about the blessings of this prosperity – one has only to think of the problem of acid rain – but it is also a deeper doubt. It is not an exaggeration to say that for a large number of people existentialism, the problem of life in the wood, doubt, the despair of Heidegger and Sartre, is present against the background of their prosperity.

Let me try to clarify all this further. Recently a whole series of publications have appeared on the development of village life. There in village life we can see clearly the problem of which I am speaking. I take as an example Jo Boer's book about the Dutch village of Zweelo in Drenthe between 1930 and 1970.[4] The author investigates many facets of country life. She writes about the development in agriculture, in family life, in teaching, in the sphere of church and religion, in the framework of social welfare and recreation and government. Her starting point is that in 1930, when the book begins, we have a simple society, a village society with little government, few machines and little education. At this time there was a clear bond between individuals and their families; the village was isolated, and dominated by a number of fixed rules for neighbourly help and marriage which people had to observe and not oppose. Alongside this picture of village life we could set the book *Montaillou*, which describes the life of a farming village at the end of the Middle Ages in the Pyrenees, on the border between France and Spain.[5] This book shows how people live close to their cattle, close to one another and also close to the church. They enjoy a kind of security, and while there may be all kinds of tensions in it, these tensions are regularly overcome. Montaillou can thus well be compared with Zweelo.

Let us return to Jo Boer's book and look more closely at some of the lines that she develops. First she speaks of agriculture: not only the husband was involved in it, but also his wife and children and usually a few people who can be reckoned as hired labourers. Where extra help was needed now and then, there were definite rules as to what was expected of neighbours. If we look to see what is left of this kind of family business after forty years we can see that as a result of mechanization the labourers have completely disappeared from the business: there are no longer any hired men. The children or members of the family hardly play any part in things. Agriculture has become a one-man business. One can speak of a kind of revolution in it. There has also been a good deal of organization: there is a milk factory and there are all sorts of co-operatives. And whereas formerly the farmer learned his work in the business itself, now all kinds of schools have grown up, and education plays a major role in agriculture. Alongside this one can think of the widespread use of fertilizers and pesticides, and we can see that here too one can speak of a revolution.

We see a similar revolution in family life. In earlier days a large family lived on the farm: grandparents lived alongside their grandchildren. One could also say that the children lived with their parents and grandparents. The housing was often primitive. There were still communal sleeping arrangements; there were no showers or baths. There was also a primitive form of welfare; midwives above all helped in deliveries. But as a result of the revolution the families have fallen apart; the grandparents no longer live on the farm, but have become independent. There are modern bedrooms and modern sanitation with a bath or shower. Advanced medical care has also grown up in the village; there are district nurses, there are inoculations, there are specialists in the neighbourhood with hospitals to which one can go. Alongside this, all kinds of organization have come into being. Husband and wife, or just the husband or just the wife, are members of all kinds of organizations: leisure organizations, women's organizations, sports organizations, music organizations, sometimes even travel organizations.

In conjunction with this revolution we see all kinds of developments emerging which we could regard as being characteristic of a modern society. There is an increase in scale: the village is no longer so isolated, life is more organized and there is increasing bureaucracy, All kinds of old rules which used to determine village life have disappeared and their place has been taken by a series of new problems, above all connected with young people. The church, which used to be at the centre of village life, has been shifted to the periphery and far less people go to it than used to. In the religious sphere, but also outside religion, there is a clear privatization of life. Of course there is still some sense of living together in the village, but the real organic society of former days is obviously disappearing. And sometimes we already see here and there a kind of nostalgia for the good old days, above all because all kinds of new illnesses, above all psychological ones, are appearing. This is a development which of course is not only to be found in Zweelo or in villages but is one familiar to all modern men and women, one that we have all experienced, and which is repeating itself all over the world. For modern society has become a universal human phenomenon. The Dutch historian Jan Romein spoke of a universal human pattern which is in process of disappearing in modern industrial society.[6] The German sociologist Arnold Gehlen has expressed the view that the development which we are experiencing in our modern society is as decisive as the development which took place earlier when human-kind moved over from a hunting and nomadic culture to a settled agricultural culture.[7]

We need to look at this development more closely and ask what the driving forces are and what are the most important consequences. In my view two phenomena are essential; the phenomenon of emancipation on the one hand and that of alienation on the other. I stress the significance of these two phenomena because they are connected with the problem of spirituality which is so important in the context of our mountain climb.

Emancipation

Let us begin by looking at emancipation. It has two aspects. First it has the aspect of coming of age with all that that entails. Deep down in men and women is the need to come of age. We already find this in Harlow's monkeys. We can also see it expressed clearly in Kant's formula that at the Enlightenment people began to emerge from a tutelage that they had brought on themselves. So for many people the French Revolution was the beginning of an attempt to come of age and gain emancipation. The American anthropologist Margaret Mead has more than once shown how in primitive societies there are always traces of latent opposition to the oldest members. We also find this concern to come of age in Jo Boer's book on Zweelo. She mentions opposition to the rules which are exercised by the elders. The remarkable thing is that the emancipation in Zweelo began when youth work was instituted. It is as it were through youth work that new possibilities arise within the village community. We see how a whole pattern of norms of courtship and marriage, living together, bringing up children, recreation, comes into being. And the important thing is that the movement is in the direction of autonomy, of freedom, of the possibility of making decisions for oneself. So deep down in human beings there is a need for independence, for being free in life and not remaining dependent.

The second aspect of emancipation is that people have a need to be able to get to know the other element in their life, the alien, the unknown, and by learnng about it to come to control it. This other element is first of all the nature which confronts us, and then the life that comes upon us which we do not know. Finally it is the fate that is thrust upon us. For us that other element is always alien, and something that is alien is in the first place threatening: it evokes anxiety. In primitive society an alien is therefore always threatening. If people are to be able to live, they must control what threatens them. That is the way in which magic comes into being. Magic is an attempt to control the unknown, fate, the future, sometimes nature. This magic later gives rise to science. Science emerges from the need to get to know the other and above all to control it. Human beings have a powerful instrument for that: their understanding. Understanding leads to science and this science is a means of domination. Through science people make an attempt to exercise power and be independent, to begin to organize and programme, and so to struggle towards independence, in order in this way, as the book of Genesis puts it, to become as like gods. We can see this need for emancipation throughout Zweelo. Agriculture has developed in this direction all along the line. We find the same direction in teaching, in health care, in family planning. No one wants to remain dependent; everyone wants to be independent and exercise control.

So we see how in this aspect the need for independence plays a major role. This finds a kind of confirmation in the need to be powerful, the need to be able to exercise power. At the same time this introduces a new element, that of alienation.

Alienation

This alienation also has two aspects. The first is that the young are alienated from the old because they break away from the rules which the old have always followed and which they would also like their children to follow. However, the children want to go their own way and as a result they have less contact with their parents; indeed there is even dissension. There is less concern to ask advice. Perhaps, too, there is no longer the need to do that: one always knows better. And as a result between children and parents there slowly develops a kind of indifference, a kind of alienation. The bond between young and old is undermined and eroded; this is expressed most clearly by the fact that the older ones go to live apart and thus young and old no longer share the same house, the same farmstead. But this alienation goes even deeper: that is the second aspect. It leads to an erosion of the security which hitherto had characterized a good deal of life. In her book Jo Boer describes how the farmer in old Zweelo had a basic security in his land, his family and a village community.[8] Now, she says, all three elements of this basic security have been attacked in the transition from one form of society to another. And she goes on: 'So is it surprising that the farmer in 1970 in some respects has become insecure?' This insecurity is coupled with negative feelings. So it is an expression of anxiety, anxiety about the future, anxiety about possible consequences of one's own actions, anxiety about the unknown, the alien modern world. And there are also feelings of frustration, the feeling of not being able to achieve what you want to achieve, and a lack of self-confidence. These, Jo Boer says, are some of the negative feelings of a person in a situation of insecurity. The question 'Am I doing it right?' and the complaint 'Whatever I do, it doesn't work out', arise daily in connection with agriculture, the upbringing of children and village life. So there is an erosion, an undermining of the original security. And from what Jo Boer says a new kind of threat comes into being. People become anxious, they have the feeling that they are no longer in control. They are aware that the independence that has been built up is vulnerable. They find

57

themselves alone, faced with a kind of void in their lives. So the lack of trust arises through a lack of security. People need trust and security above all.

A number of clear factors play a role in this process. In village life we see the growth of organization and bureaucracy, the increase in mechanization, economizing and the increasing role of money. That means that alienation consists in no longer having contact with what can be called the primary reality of life. There is an alienation from the community but also an alienation from oneself, and often also an alienation from one's children, from one's wife, from one's friends. That means that alienation leads to isolation.

We can draw all kinds of conclusions from this, and I suppose that all of us can recognize ourselves in this process. A first conclusion is that we have two needs: a need for independence and a need for security. We see that there is a living connection between these two. The growth towards independence happens on the basis of security: the two are intrisically related. The person who has not known any security will not know any real independence either. That also means that the boundaries can be shifted. They depend on the time of a person's life, his or her upbringing, on cultural patterns, particular stress situations, the degree to which a person can be more independent and the degree to which he or she needs more security.

My second conclusion is that in any situation people are therefore ambivalent. They look for both security and independence in life at the same time. They need to feel secure and at the same time to do things in order to be free, to control themselves and their lives. That means that men and women are in principle uncertain and never definitively overcome their uncertainty. That is also implicit in Terrien's views, when he talks about the elusive presence: people need presence, but this presence is always elusive. This means that at heart we are always uncertain, insecure. One can say that religion and especially spirituality are an answer to this situation.

My third conclusion is that we can get a better view from here of the development of modern society. In Zweelo the contrast was still simple: there were two types of society, the agricultural and the modern. Elsewhere the reality is more complicated. We see that agrarian society usually first leads to an urban society, the society of the small town in which there is more independence but still sufficient of a community feeling not to allow this independence to turn into isolation. What we now experience, however, is that both agricultural society and this urban society are developing in the direction of what has been called abstract society, a society which is characterized by organization, by bureaucracy and by a far-reaching alienation.

A good deal is said these days about the welfare state. In this welfare state the process of individualization has progressed even further, for the individual receives the help that he or she gets from the bureaucracy, and therefore it comes as part of a process of alienation. Moreover this welfare state also has a number of negative features (of course, alongside a number of positive ones): drug abuse, the increase in the divorce rate, the collapse of community life (in other words the fact that the rules of community life are no longer observed), the rise of the youth problem, all the phenomena which are connected with alienation.

What I have just said is an attempt at orientation with the help of sociology. What we experience as human beings and also what we call our spirituality is thus part of a process in our society. As we live, act and think we are also a product of this process. It is a process which is characterized by privatization. This confronts poeople with the void, with emptiness, with the abyss. However, at the same time we have to note that this process is a challenge for us to respond to; it is therefore not just to be accepted passively but a call to find an answer and seek a new way for our society. The question is whether we can transcend this confrontation with the void.

Psychology

Alongside the sociological map there is the psychological map. What do we find when we try to read this map? The answer can be given relatively simply. Psychology similarly shows that there are two central aspects to human development, in this case to our psychological development. One can therefore talk of emancipation and alienation from the beginning. We see this again with Harlow's monkeys: these monkeys feel secure with their mother-substitutes. They are curious; they venture into the cage, but there they are threatened. They retreat, look for renewed security and then go off again. They are able as it were to control themselves, and also want to control that other. So here too there is a development, a psychological development, with emancipation on the one hand and alienation on the other: emancipation from and alienation from the mother. Here, however, the emphasis is on the positive side. Both alienation and emancipation are necessary for achieving independence. Moreover with human beings a special element begins to play a part here, the element of a possible repression of feelings. People can repress feelings of anxiety, of dependence, of anger. By repression they can achieve a kind of inauthentic independence; this is coupled with an alienation from society and even alienation from the mother. It seems that as a result of the repression of feelings no real security is any longer possible with the mother. Moreover the parents (e.g. the mother) can often fail to give themselves any real security: they hold the child too firmly or they push it away. A good example of this is what Emmy van Overeen says in her book about Tessa. The consequence is that there can be no question of a real emancipation: this becomes inauthentic. It has no basis in the security of society, but lays all the stress on privacy. Political extremism and certain youth problems can be the result. This is an emancipation which does not lead to authentic independence and also has the consequence that alienation which can basically be healthy becomes unhealthy. Such an alienation can go very deep: in that case it does not keep a healthy distance from the other, is devoid of any feeling of belonging to the other, of being together with him or her. In our society we see people in apartment blocks living physically close to one another but being psychologically alienated, indeed often living in fear of one another. So we can say that the psychological map to some degree supplements the sociological map.

Our conclusion can be that people need to have a dynamic experience of freedom and community in which, as I said, the boundaries between the two can be shifted. To be adult in the psychological sense means to retain one's stance when the two poles of freedom and community begin to move apart. It thus means being able to be alone without becoming anxious: one has self-confidence. We can also say that being adult means knowing real feelings of freedom and of belonging. This is where the challenge that I mentioned at the end of the discussion of the sociological map becomes clearer. The reaction to the void, in other words the reaction to the basic problems of our human existence, can be positive only if we are authentic individuals. In other words, spirituality is dealing with oneself authentically in the great uncertainties of our existence.

Philosophy

Finally we come to discuss the philosophical map. Here I am thinking particularly of existentialist philosophy. I shall not repeat what I said earlier, but simply bring out one important point briefly.

Heidegger talks about the pull in human existence towards the 'they'. For him that includes alienation from ourselves, from our 'being there'. He asks how we can achieve authenticity. However, he does not make it clear how that can happen. He talks about a challenge of the conscience that summons us to authenticity. But this is reminiscent of Baron von Münchhausen, who had to get himself out of the morass by his hair. I think that psychology can take us further here. This shows us that for authenticity, real community with others is important. People achieve authenticity through a guru, through a teacher, and in the very first years of life through parents, mother and father. That means that the way to authenticity is never purely rational. Philosophers seldom reflect on the significance of the other for philosophizing. But the other is often implicitly present in philosophy: in the form of a colleague or friends, of pupils or of an audience. In Greece philosophers were always trained in schools; in other words, philosophy is essentially always a kind of conversation, a dialogue.

We learn from Kohut how the presence of the mother, of the other person, is an essential element in our human existence. The mother is initially present in a primal symbiosis, after that as a mirror and finally as a matrix of empathy. For philosophy, too, it is the case that the presence of the other is the basis on which one can arrive at authenticity. For Kohut, authenticity also leads to creativity. Paul Tillich says in his book *The Courage to Be* that this courage to be oneself is based on participation, on being part of a greater whole.[9]

Conclusion

So our conclusion may be that the wood in which we are wandering has an entrance: we enter the wood through the family in which we grow up, through contacts with parents and especially with our mothers. And we may conclude that the wood, the labyrinth, also has a way, the way of the other, of the group, the people, the church. Finally we ask: does the wood also have a way out? We shall examine that question in detail in the next chapter.

In this chapter we have looked more closely at the situation of modern society and at the same time considered the problem of spirituality. As men and women we are on a journey and we have also brought provisions with us on this journey. These provisions consist of basic trust, the basic trust with which we begin the journey. And on this journey we also find provisions on the way through the labyrinth in certain sources, the small communities that we discover there. So even in the labyrinth there are still forces to counter the forces of alienation. My view is that in these provisions we find support for going further.

As we go on we in fact discover two things. First, in the wood there are patches of what Heidegger has called 'Lichtung', clearings.[10] What can he have mean by that? I believe that for him these are moments when we are closer to ourselves, and therefore are closer to the mystery. That can happen through a poem, a painting or a piece of music; it can also happen through a conversation, through meditation, through going to a church service. Then there are 'clearings'. We are not yet in a position to say that we have arrived at faith; that we clearly see and know things and that we take a decision on the basis of that; these are rather moments when we see something and have ideas, when our horizons are enlarged. Perhaps these are the peak experiences that Maslow talks about.[11]

The second thing that we discover is that there are others alongside us. These others are not strangers but companions, who are sharing the journey with us, with whom we have a particular bond and who therefore also provide some illumination in our life. In company with these others we relive the family in which we grew up and as a result of this we are detached from our egocentrism. We begin to discover perspectives on deeper possibilities in our existence, perspectives of solidarity, trust, confidence in one another. These are perspectives that we find worked out in the philosophy of Levinas. In the following chapters I shall have to say more about them.

So a way has appeared through the wood, a way which begins somewhere and which points towards a way out, a way which as it were opens up a perspective beyond the fumbling in the darkness which is what existentialism amounts to, the view of a sphere above the treeline. We shall go on to explore above the treeline in the next chapter.

* five *

Above the Treeline

How far have we got on our journey? We left the village of our youth, and with it the security of a faith with its church and its sacred order. I said earlier that in its development humanity has left behind Jan Romein's 'universal human pattern'. With Samuel Terrien we saw that the security of human life is precarious. The life of Israel and of the Christian community was secured in a particular divine presence. However, the essential thing about this presence was that it was elusive. The fundamental presence in human life, that of one's parents and of God, is always elusive. So there is a tension in human existence, a tension between security on the one hand and isolation on the other.

After that, our journey took us into the wood. There we were confronted with one pole of human existence, the pole of insecurity. We saw how the existentialist philosophy of Heidegger reflected on this insecurity. We noted that life can be a labyrinth, that people can feel thrown into the world, that they have a sense of going along 'Holzwege', paths which do not lead anywhere and come to dead ends, and that they see death as the only way out of life.

On our journey through the wood we also consulted maps, sociological and psychological maps, and we saw how these two disciplines teach us that in the history of human life here on earth there is emanicipation and alienation and as a result – in Erikson's words – a basic trust stands over against a basic mistrust. Human beings are always ambivalent: they follow two courses in life at the same time. They seek security and at the same time they seek freedom and independence. In the encounter with the other they keep trying to discover something of their former security and at the same time in their freedom they reach out for self-realization.

Now we have emerged from the wood above the treeline. There life takes on new perspectives. The summit of the mountain again comes into view, though it is still a long way away. The terrain over which we have to go becomes gradually rougher: it is cold on the mountain slope, cold in the fierce sun which is shining. Far down below, every now and then we can see the village. The paths that we have to tread are not always clearly visible. Others have gone before us on these paths, and here and there we see indications of how they went and in which direction they point us. We are reminded of stories from the Old Testament and in connection with them of the views of those modern theologians who speak of an exodus. In the Old Testament we read how the exodus provoked two reactions among those who took part in it. In the first place there was one of nostalgia: in the wilderness people longed for the fleshpots of Egypt. They again sought security, the security of rites, of symbols, of the holy order, and they tried to find this in worship of the golden calf. This is a nostalgia for Jan Romein's universal human pattern, for a 'whole' world. It is also a nostalgia for comfort. We are not far from flight into the 'they' of which Heidegger speaks, and close to what Barth means by his concept of religion.[1]

Many phenomena in religion and the church in our time are understandable in terms of this nostalgia. Behind many of them there is anxiety. One can keep hearing people ask, 'Where will all this lead to?' They are clearly anxious about the future. And because of all this anxiety they conjure up all kinds of gurus. We hear bishops and popes make forthright statements and old and new regulations and rules are prescribed for us. People cultivate peak experiences, they seek salvation in new groups. All this is an expression of nostalgia for the fleshpots of Egypt.

However, a second reaction is possible. Moses spoke in his way not of comfort but of challenge. People can feel challenged to become themselves, to live as emancipated men and women, really to breathe the fresh air here above the treeline. Up here they can look around and discover what tasks are imposed on them and

65

what questions are put to them. I was once involved in an experiment which the Roman Catholic church organized in a new suburb in Boxtel in Brabant.[2] This experiment was carried out under the supervision of the diocese of 's-Hertogenbosch and by the Tilburg theological faculty. They wanted to investigate how people would practise their faith in a new suburb where there was as yet no church building and how they could ask questions of the church on the basis of their faith. Two ministers, a pastor and a pastoral worker, were appointed there and they worked to make contact with the people from this district. What emerged from this experiment?

First, it became clear that people attached importance to the ancient sacraments, and that therefore sacraments like baptism and confirmation had to find a place in this new suburb. That was one thing. The other was that they seemed to need to get together in discussion groups and talk over the situation in the new suburb. Often they had come from other places in the Netherlands. In these conversations it emerged that they felt a desire to get rid of their past and go their own way, to experiment with new things in their life. But what also emerged was that when these conversations touched on deep matters, the very people who were concerned to get rid of the past and to be open to new perspectives also found that they were confronted with themselves, with deeper questions, deeper personal realities. They began to talk about their isolation, about death. Nor did things stop at this confrontation; these people also dwelt on what one could call the deeper realities of this world. They dwelt on the problems which this world presents to us, the problems of war and suffering and what emerged as the basic question in these conversations: how can we believe, as men and women in this modern world?

One can say that in these conversations we come upon the situation that we find in the letters which Bonhoeffer wrote from prison during the war. As is well known, Bonhoeffer is the pioneer of a new, radical theology. When we read his letters, we find this double reaction to the exodus, a rebellion against nostalgia and at the same time the experience of life as a challenge. With Bonhoeffer there is first of all an opposition to nostalgia. He says:

'I really cannot believe (though perhaps I might still want to) in a God who is worshipped as creator and Father, who is a God of the gaps that we find in this world.' For him this God was a guarantor of an ordered and in many respects bourgeois society, a society which Bonhoeffer had come to know so well in his parents' home.

The second thing is that he experiences life as a challenge. He says that we shall have to learn to live – and evidently he felt this as a challenge – as though God did not exist: *Etsi deus non daretur*. He argues that God is absent from the modern world. God is a God who has withdrawn from this world: that means that he points us towards living in this world. So we live as it were in the fresh air, in the awareness of having to be independent and therefore of having to bear responsibility.

Our journey above the treeline is like this exodus. Above the treeline we get into a harsher climate: it is colder there; sometimes there is mist and sometimes there are storms. Certainly there is a good deal of sun, and there are wide views above the treeline, but we are unprotected there: the path is difficult and hard; we have to climb, and it leads past all kinds of crevasses. There are no longer any houses where we can live safely; we have to live in tents.

Let me make a brief observation in passing. In modern times we find the idea that the church, too, is a tent. In line with the stories in the book of Exodus that mention the tabernacle, which is a tent and not yet a temple, people today can represent the church as being a tent. In Ronchamps in the south of France the French architect Le Corbusier built an impressive church to which he gave the form of a tent.

Life above the treeline is often also dangerous. We have to rope up, to tie ourselves to one another in order to get further. Life there can only be experienced as teamwork; the individual cannot do anything without the help of others. To travel alone is dangerous. And as well as the team we also need a guide, a guide who knows the way and who will lead the group, using a compass so as not to lose direction. Films of people climbing in the mountains above the treeline give an impression of the dangers and of the need for collaboration. They also give an impression of the perseverance that is necessary. The summit aimed at is there, but it is often guarded by sheer cliff faces, or it is in mist and always seems a long way away.

Some things seem to me to be important if we are to be aware of what is asked of us above the treeline. In the first place there is the knowledge that it is no longer possible to go back below the treeline. We might possibly get back again from the wood, but from here it is impossible. I am reminded of a book written by Tjeu van den Berk entitled *Beyond the Point of No Return*.[3] In this book van den Berk, who did his doctorate on Bonhoeffer, put forward a number of ideas in connection with a radical theology or better a radical catechesis, in other words a radical form of religious instruction. His basic idea is that in catechetics, in religious education, we have gone down a dead end, and he gives a radical analysis of the situation. He wants to do theology with a sense of helplessness and ignorance. He confronts us constantly with statements by Nietzsche, Freud and Marx and accuses us of still continuing to think in too half-hearted a way. So we can say that to go further above the treeline is to be willing and able to see the radical character of our world situation. That means also being willing to learn from existentialism, for existentialism has tried to demonstrate the radical nature of our world situation.

The second important thing is that we need one another in this journey above the treeline. I have already spoken in terms of roping up. We have to help one another, we sometimes have to think together and do things together. Making progress above the treeline is making progress in a team. I think that is also what feminists are discovering at present when they experience what sisterhood means for them. By going together in a team, in the first place we get a feeling of security. The team provides a degree of security. In the team we reactivate the feelings we used to have in our family. As a result, a kind of basic trust emerges in the team.

Secondly, we discover that we can and must discuss things with one another. We have to work out the way with one another and thus clarify our position together. That means at the same time that we deepen our relationship with one another so that it becomes mutual commitment, that we feel mutually bound to one another. William Hamilton, the author of *The New Essence of Christianity*, says that we modern men are really like displaced persons round a camp fire, telling stories to one another there.[4] Is that not the situation which we experience with one another in the team above the treeline?

The third important thing is the value and significance of solidarity. Roping ourselves together means that we know that we can and must stick to one another, that we must do things for one another, that we support one another and bear burdens for one another. We must inspire one another and also must comfort one another.

Existentialism, the philosophy of the wood, laid emphasis on the isolation, the individuality of human life. So according to Karl Jaspers, Kierkegaard and Nietzsche – the forerunners of existentialism – were people who lived on the basis of a deep solitude, an isolation that we again find stressed in Heidegger.[5] It is doubtless the case that the modern world leads to individualization, but in the depths of human life there is also already the awareness of a relationship. So the philosophy of Levinas is built on the notion that people look towards one another and in looking towards one another build up a relationship. We get the impression that the individual comes from a family and that he or she enters the world from that family supported by a matrix, a source of empathy.

In the previous chapter we saw that in our day we have arrived at a particular point in a psychological and historical process. It is good to remember that at this point. This is a process which is characterized by emancipation on the one hand and alienation on the other. One can also define it in sociological terms as a process in which humanity moves over from Romein's 'the universal human pattern' to the pattern of a technological society. In terms of a psychological process this is a development which is characterized by a departure from the family, withdrawal from the influence of parents, and a quest for autonomy, for independence. From a historical perspective it consists in the development from

69

a primitive, feudal tribal community which, as far as we can look back in history, forms the beginning of human society, to a modern welfare state. At present, however, this modern welfare state is clearly in a crisis. In this situation the question arises: what has happened to humankind? This is the question which Fortmann raised. On the one hand people have become freer, they have emancipated themselves, they are more independent. But at the same time they are more isolated in this process: they experience the insecurity of life. They feel threatened in a particular way: they have become people in search of basic trust. Moreover at the end of the twentieth century we are now aware that this process of emancipation and alienation has accelerated. Our experiences have become much more burdensome. We have two world wars behind us. We can look back on fantastic progress in science and industry. But at the same time we are experiencing a crisis of our capitalist system because we can no longer solve the problem of unemployment on the one hand or the problems of the Third World on the other. We all live with the recollection of concentration camps. And we can see how at present two great world powers are in a state of confrontation, with an incredibly large arsenal of nuclear weapons. We really all live in a paradox with power on the one hand and powerlessness to arrive at meaningful humanity in the world on the other.

Getting above the treeline means that we begin to see humanity in perspective. When from this perspective we think about the problems of a modern spirituality which can speak to our world, we become aware that we are confronted with some fundamental experiences. In the first place there is the difficulty of believing in God in the old way. Heidegger and Sartre say that there is no sacred, transcendent order: God is dead, or God does not exist. In modern theology we find traces of this spirit of the age in someone like Bonhoeffer, who writes that God abandons this world and is not a God of the gaps. These traces are clear in the 'death of God theology' which emerged in the 1960s and in which we find the influence of Nietzsche. The message is not completely clear, but there are certain figures, like Dorothee Sölle, who try to develop the basic ideas of this 'death of God theology' in a new way so that it speaks to the present. We also find an example of this in Edward Schillebeeckx's book *God is New Every Moment*. At the end of the conversations it records Schillebeeckx produces a psalm prayer with the title 'Do not Fear', in which some characteristic sentences appear. For example: 'Are you a God at hand, and not a God far off? Truly, you are a hidden God. You are ready to be sought. Do I look for you in chaos? But the poor and needy seek water and there is none. May you find people, Lord, who work for justice. Lord, I believe, help my unbelief! I am a poor fool, Lord, teach me how to pray!'[6]

Thus in our day spirituality is increasingly characterized by the sense of a world abandoned by God. As a result, a fundamental doubt has arisen in the minds of many people. They cannot suppress the question whether belief in God in a godforsaken world is not perhaps a projection. The problem of projection is often and urgently discussed, especially in the Netherlands. It seems as though God used to be present in a sacred order, in the church, in history: there was a time when Dutch people believed in the trinity of God, Netherlands and Orange; other people had a similar trinity. It seemed also as though God was present in bourgeois society. Now, however, the accent has come increasingly to be placed on the elusiveness of God, on God's incomprehensibility, on God's absence, on the question whether the former belief was not really in fact an illusion. I would say that God is not completely absent; God is also present in our modern society, but present as it were in the distance. He is present as a recollection of former upbringing, as a father-image against which people can fight, as the desire that they have for healing and meaning, as an archetype, as a magician. Here I am thinking of modern astrology or modern charismatic movments. He is also present in the nostalgia of all kinds of fundamentalists.

But despite all this, the dominant factor in our society remains the experience of elusiveness. That means that our world is secularized, godforsaken. The human situation in our time is comparable to that of Job. However, for Job God was still present as a partner, as one who could be invoked and with whom Job could therefore enter into a dialogue, whereas in our modern world God has become distant and vague, and people ask whether he really exists. This elusiveness of God has two major consequences. The first is that human beings are emancipated: they are free. They have become responsible for themselves and responsible for the world. That is the idea which dominates Bonhoeffer's thinking.[7] At the same time humankind lives with a challenge. We have incredible technological potential: we can land on the moon, carry on war in space; we have invented computers, we can control nuclear energy; medical science has made unimaginable progress and as a result of biochemistry we are penetrating the deepest mysteries of life. Human beings have never been so challenged by new possibilities as they are today. The second consequence is the discovery of suffering. Of course suffering has always been there, but formerly it was incorporated into the sacred transcendent order that dominated the world. For example, men and women experienced suffering as punishment for a sin or it was seen as an expression of God's will. There were also those who saw suffering as a lesson which had to be learned in life or as a necessary shadow cast because of the light. It was thought impossible to experience the light without the shadow of suffering. But in a godforsaken world suffering is shown to be a scandal. It appears as a riddle, as a disruption of creation, and also as a sign of human failure. In a famous study Herman Wiersinga asked whether it was possible to be reconciled to suffering.[8] He was thinking of the cancer patients with whom he was confronted. His answer was that it was not possible. This is a fundamentally different experience of suffering from that mentioned above. Camus defends the notion that suffering is the absurd in this world and that we must therefore rebel against this world.[9] We find kindred ideas in Schillebeeckx in the book I mentioned earlier. In it Schillebeeckx says: 'I can situate a certain amount of suffering. But there is such an excess of suffering and evil that I cannot situate it at all.' 'How do you pray, then?', he was asked. 'I am despairing. Sometimes I simply swear, I swore when I heard that Oscar Romero had been murdered in San Salvador. I was angry. But then I thought: well, that is also a form of prayer, so long as it doesn't remain just swearing.' 'How should it continue, then?',

Schillebeeckx was asked. 'It shouldn't continue with your saying: God must have an intention here, but rather with your saying: we are still in God's hands, even in grim situations like this one. This terrible event isn't the last word.'[10] When Dorothee Sölle talks about suffering in her book, she says that suffering makes people dumb.[11]

In all modern radical theologies we find that people live on the basis of a confrontation with suffering that can no longer be fitted into a higher order. In his book on *The New Essence of Christianity*, William Hamilton used here an image of living in a house in which we have what he calls stormwindows, double glazing against the storm outside. But, he says, in the theology of Karl Barth the windows which open on suffering are without double glazing.[12] We are looking for a double glazing for these storwindows. One can even say that this experience of suffering increases the sense of godforsakenness in this world. People can also feel homeless, as Hamilton says elsewhere in his book. The experience of Christ on the cross, asking God in his suffering 'Why have you forsaken me?', is the evidence of this. This experience of godforsakenness in suffering is a problem about which there is much discussion at present.[13] In the West suffering has never really been an important theme of theological discussion. It often seems as though guilt were the central theme of theology.[14] In the East things are different. In Buddhism suffering is the central theme of human thought. As far as the West is concerned we can note that the great questions of existentialism, of living in the wood, appear within theology, within belief. They are the questions of meaninglessness, death, isolation, freedom. When we speak of a modern Christian spirituality, that must be a spirituality which can go into these questions in a positive, liberating way. So the question arises, is that possible?

The second thing that seems to me to be fundamental to the present situation and thus central to a modern spirituality is that we come from a bourgeois society, in other words a society which is characterized by an order, a sense of security, a desire for emancipation, a basic trust. Paul Tillich has described bourgeois society as the society of finitude resting on itself.[15] However, we have to say that much has been suppressed under this finitude resting in itself. Has not the problem of death been concealed and suppresed in the bourgeois society with a tabu?[16] And sexuality?

Now above the treeline we are confronted with a great gap, with the void. We discover that there is no God of the gaps, we discover the abyss of suffering, and alongside that we discover our neighbour, our fellow human being. So we ask whether in that case there is no sacred order, whether there is only capitalist exploitation, whether there is only a racist desire for power and a continuing collapse of society. So we ask whether there is no security but only insecurity, only meaninglessness. Is there no trust but only mistrust, only 'making the most of things', only alienation? These are the great questions which arise from the crisis of bourgeois society and which call for reflection. What are these questions basically about?

I think that existentialism gives us an answer to this last question. Existentialism has shown us that people's attention is focussed on the world. We live in a world which we organize, manipulate and order. As children we learn to eat with a knife and fork. Later we divide out our work and organize our spare time. So – and this is Heidegger's basic thought – we always live in an organized world. We surround ourselves with a society which creates order and in this order we feel secure. This is the life of the 'they'. In our everydayness the world around us is a source of security. Is that not really what bourgeois society provides and what Tillich means by his 'finitude resting on itself'?

Above the treeline we then discover that there are gaps in this world. In the wood, existentialism has already confronted us with the problem of death, with the problem that there is no foundation to life. Above the treeline there are two gaps which we find in our world. We discover our fellow men and women alongside us and we discover the suffering in our own existence. We shall see that these two cannot be separated.

In the first place we discover our fellow men and women. The basic notion of Levinas' philosophy is that our fellow men and women, the others in our existence, open up a gap. Our neighbour comes to us, looks at us and in his or her look there is a call. That means that these people do not fit into our world. They are not objects that we can organize and control; they are free. And in their freedom they come into our world. The consequence of this is that they disturb our attitude to the world. Through our fellow men and women we break new ground in our existence; new perspectives are opened up to us. The important thing is that these people make us insecure. We can no longer use the usual categories that we use in dealing with things in this world. We now become those who are addressed by our fellow men and women; we are challenged. It is as though we come to stand before an abyss, before a gap in our lives.

Secondly there is the gap, the abyss, of suffering. In his existentialist philosophy Karl Jaspers speaks of boundary situations.[17] Suffering is such a boundary situation. It is a situation which we cannot control, which we cannot master. We can only enter into it and investigate it.

A few years ago I took part in a conference in Pullach in Germany,[18] where with theologians and psychologists we studied the problems, above all the practical problems, of suffering. It was a first reconnaissance of an area which is still difficult and undeveloped. In the same way we can see the books by Dorothee Sölle and Wiersinga about suffering as a reconnaissance. At this conference I came to see that the first human reaction to suffering, to illness, to one's own distress or that of others, to famine, is: 'Something must happen here, something must be done here.' Suffering always presents us with a challenge, above all with a challenge to our technological capacity. In particular in modern times we have many ways of attacking suffering. The comfort which we give to people in their suffering therefore often consists in attempting to do something for them. However, on closer inspection it emerges that suffering always affects people at a deeper level, a different level from that of action. And at this level lie the great problems which suffering poses to us. Suffering is a riddle, and something of a mystery. It is always a threat, a danger to our lives. There is something intangible and therefore also something incomprehensible about it. Camus rightly speaks of the absurd. I myself believe that we can go a stage further and say that suffering is experienced as a enemy. It tears us away from the life that we have experienced hitherto, the life that provided a degree of security and that was a warm society in which we felt secure. Now suffering enters our life as an enemy and tears us from it. What is happening here? We noticed with Harlow's monkeys that whenever they were faced with a threat in the cage, they felt isolated and anxiety developed. That is the suffering that enters their life. What they then do is to rush back to their mothers. With their mothers they are secure, with their mothers there is warmth and because of that the pain and suffering become tolerable. We see the same thing with children. When a child falls down and get hurt it feels alone. It goes to its mother, and being with its mother generates a kind of security, a warmth, as a result of which it is possible to bear the pain. The pain then becomes tolerable. It does not disappear, but becomes open to discussion. Here we might think of Dorothee Sölle's comment that suffering in the first instance makes people dumb, and needs a language if it is to be discussed.[19] It is the presence of the mother, the presence of the other person, which makes possible an acceptance of pain, which makes it bearable because of the security provided by the group with which the person is involved. Suffering of itself produces isolation. In that isolation suffering become intolerable. There it remains a riddle, an enemy.

I said earlier that suffering and one's fellow men and women are inseparable. Can we say more about this relationship between suffering and our fellow men and women? It is a twofold relationship. First, as Levinas says, the other person's face presents us with a call. We are challenged, summoned to do something. However, I think that the other person's face does even more. Here we have the presence of the other person which removes our isolation: the other person can look on us with understanding, as a mother welcomes her lonely child with understanding. We are people who suffer, and because of that – as Levinas argues – others can do something for us. They can break through our isolation by their understanding. It is increasingly being concluded that the presence of the therapist has a good deal to do with the effect of psychotherapy.[20] What is being said here is that the presence of others in our lives and the understanding they show to us have a mystery of their own. With an authentic relationship between two people something comes into being like a resonance betwen the one and the other. The other person also suffers, he or she enters into my suffering, feels it with me, shares in it, as a mother shares in the suffering of her child. That also means that the mother allows heself to be made insecure, opens herself to the child. Is that not what Carl Rogers means when he says that authenticity is an important element in the effect of psychotherapy?[21] When we see things in this way it means that people who are open and understanding are combining two activities. On the one hand they are being themselves and on the other hand they are simultaneously identifying with the other person.

This produces a kind of polarity of nearness and distance, with an associated sense that in suffering and sharing in suffering we come closer to authentic living. I recall a conversation with someone who had experienced great suffering and who said, 'Now I've grown up, now I know what life involves. I'm no longer so naive, I'm as it were adult, I've become more authentic.' That means that while there is the gap of suffering in our lives, it is also possible to enter into this gap. That means bearing suffering, and sustaining it. That is true of our own personal suffering, but also of communal suffering. People can support one another in suffering. By making it possible to discuss suffering (see Sölle) people come closer to one another and support one another. Is not that perhaps what we understand by love? I think that an important conclusion needs to be drawn from this, namely that in love people transcend suffering. In other words, in the reality of their everyday life they are confronted with a void, with a gap, but they can transcend this confrontation in love. There is a disclosure of another reality, one of freedom, independence, courage and hope. This disclosure arises in the possibility of our being open to ourselves and able to receive what is given us; in other words there is an activity which leads to passiveness. This is what Schillebeeckx meant by 'giving credit'. One could put it another way and say that our fellow human being becomes a guide for us who lifts us over the crevasse, who bring us into the light and gives us ground under our feet.

The third fundamental element in our situation is the question whether it is possible to experience God in a new way. I think that it is, and I have two supporting arguments. I am well aware that we must not be too hasty in attempting to salvage faith or religion in our time.

My first argument is that this disclosure is essentially the same as the disclosure people used to experience in relation to their parents. The parents supported their children in the confrontation with the void, the nothingness, and in so doing disclosed life and happiness to them. They became as it were God for their children. It is commensurate with this that Dorothee Sölle says that God has no other hands than our hands. We can also say that God's hands can be detected in our hands. Here we come close to the thought expressed by Levinas that traces of God are to be found in the reality of human life.[22]

My second argument is that as men and women of our time we have a place in a history, a communal history in which we have experienced certain disclosures, as a result of which we have come to believe in the presence of a redeeming God. Here I am thinking of the history of Israel, of the life of Jesus Christ, of the history of the Christian church, and therefore of the stories that we find in the Old and New Testaments. As we now live, we live in a society the mystery of which is its relationship to those disclosures that we find in the Old and New Testaments. The basic thought which is alive in this community is that God is present in history through Moses, through the prophets, through Jesus Christ, through the martyrs and through the Reformers. We come to see that we are on a journey on which we are led by guides who can disclose the other reality to us. I would stress that these experiences are in line with those which we had with our parents. In one sense they are an articulation of those experiences, but they go far beyond them. In all this, Christ is the central figure. I want to say something about the place which Christ occupies here. We shall go more closely into it in the next chapter.

Faith in Christ originally fits into a particular religious paradigm, in the sense in which Kuhn talks of paradigms.[23] One can also say that it fits into the universal human pattern which I have referred to several times before. This paradigm has the features of a Near Eastern pattern of life. Central to it is a God who is father and king, who lives in a palace and who as father feels himself responsible for the people of which he is king. He also feels responsible for people on the periphery. It is in keeping with this Near Eastern idea of the king that the divinity, the king, is sometimes present in this world incognito. One might think of the stories in the *Thousand and One Nights*. He wants to justice to prevail in his kingdom. So the earthly king represents the God who is father and king and in Israel that leads to a particular royal family which is represented by David, who is the representative of Yahweh. From this royal family one day a Messiah, a new anointed, a new king, will emerge. That, briefly, is the paradigm that we find in the Old and New Testaments.

This paradigm remained the basis for the great doctrinal structure which was produced by the first councils of the Christian church: the doctrine of the Trinity is incorporated in it.[24] The question must be raised to what degree the paradigm can still be of use in our day, now that we and our society have abandoned the 'universal human pattern'. I think that this was the focal point of the process against Schillebeeckx in Rome. I believe that we can argue that we are experiencing a transformation of the old paradigm, and that in this transformation we begin by putting the life of Jesus, the view of Jesus as Messiah, at the centre. We also find the beginnings of this in Dorothee Sölle's book *Christ the Representative*, a book in which she refers back to certain ideas in Bonhoeffer. The same line is taken by van Peursen, who argues that we are moving from an ontological period with a paradigm of its own to a functional period, with another paradigm.[25] Here I would like to make some provisional comments: we shall go into the issue more deeply in the next chapter. In the New Testament Christ is worshipped as God's servant, who must suffer and who is willing to suffer. He has been seen as God; there has been a disclosure in his life and work. Now he enters into suffering; he takes the cross upon himself. Taking the cross upon himself raises enormous questions for those who believe in him. However, two things become clear through his cross. The first is that God does not do away with suffering. Suffering remains an absurdity in this world. But God is present in our suffering, as a mother is present in the life and suffering of her child, with a presence by which she overcomes the darkness in the life of her child. God stretches out a hand to us in our suffering, in our darkness, on the cross.

The second thing that becomes clear is that suffering is a scandal, a stumbling block; it remains something that runs contrary to the will of God. Suffering in this world must therefore be challenged; it is the great hindrance to men and women on their way to the kingdom of God. We can say that the cross is on the one hand a disclosure of love, and on the other hand a way which is open to us. Here we have a transformation of the paradigm. It is a transformation which fits our image of the mountain climb. We can say that Christ is our true guide, the guide on our journey. The true guide is the one who works for those for whom he is responsible, who supports them, who summons them to teamwork, and who takes on himself the suffering and the difficulty of the journey, who in this way shows and opens up the way to the summit. I shall have more to say about Christ as the guide in the next chapter.

Finally, led me make one last comment. Suffering is thus a central experience in human existence. Various responses may be made to suffering – I have already indicated them in this chapter. The response of Buddhism is that suffering is overcome when we extinguish life with its longings and its desires. The response of Marxism is that suffering is connected with the structures of this world and that we have to resist these structures in order to secure human liberation. I believe that Marxism has not really plumbed the depths of suffering, the suffering of the other, of the fellow man or woman here; it has not seen what Levinas is talking about. The Christian response is that suffering is indeed connected with the structures and that we have to rebel against these structures. But at the same time Christianity seeks to look into both the abysses I have mentioned and to enter into them. Here Christ is our guide.

* *six* *

On with the Guide

We have now come to the last chapter. We have part of the journey behind us. We began in the village in the morning, then we went through the wood and we are now above the treeline.

How do we get any further? Every now and then we get a view of the summit, but we cannot always see it: it vanishes in the mist or suddenly disappears behind the rocks. Films about mountain climbing which we see on television show how slow is the progress that climbers make above the treeline; every now and then they have to hack out a path, and sometimes they hang on ropes on the cliff faces. They are not alone; they work together and they are bound to one another by ropes. Anyone who has seen this kind of film will be aware how thoroughly climbers must prepare and how they must be able to rely on one another. We note how one goes ahead. He is the guide. He is a pioneer. He has already been to the summit; he knows the way and in a special sense he represents the group. He therefore belongs as it were in a special category; he discloses another kind of reality. Watching a film on climbing I was reminded of the posters that you could see in the London Underground during the Second World War: 'It all depends on you' and 'You depend on God'. In other words, during the war we were also roped up, bound together by ropes, but our ultimate support, our ultimate direction was of another, higher category.

We have seen that to be human means to be confronted with the void, and to believe in a presence which fills this void. We find an example of this in Harlow's monkeys, in the mother who welcomes the child. But the essential thing about this presence is that it is elusive. In other words, it is there and at the same time it is not there. Hence the father of the epileptic son in Mark 9 calls out, 'Lord, I believe, help my unbelief', and Schillebeeckx says that the nature of faith consists in giving credit. This means that believing is not a matter of knowing, of depending on a particular theory, far less of having a different, higher insight. Belief does not build on the results of a particular investigation. Nor is it a feeling, a surge of nobility, a feeling of sympathy or even a peak experience. Knowing and feeling certainly play a role, but we are closer to the essence of things when we say that believing is a decision or implies a decision. Believing means taking a particular step, it calls for a particular dedication, it involves something like a promise, a commitment. It is comparable to what I heard said about love in a course on marriage encounter. Those taking part were told that loving one another is more than knowing, more than feeling. Love, they were told, is essentially a decision: it is standing up for one another, wanting to give one another a particular credit. In confrontation with the void, three ways of doing this are visible in the Western world.

First there is the way of existentialism: we can see this clearly in Camus, who says that life is absurd. His first book was about the figure of Sisyphus, who had to roll a rock up a hill. However, as he got towards the top, he felt the rock slipping. It rolled back down to the bottom and he had to begin all over again. In this view life is a burden, a hopeless burden.

The second way is that of Catholic spirituality. We noted in Terrien how a very specific line could be seen in the religion of Israel. Terrien calls this the line of glory. On this line the eye is the central organ; it is the line which involves the use of images in worship. Jerusalem is the centre of this type of religion. In it a major role is played by the temple, the priesthood and the royal dynasty. There is a clear difference from the prophetic line, where the stress lies on the ear and the name. Terrien stresses that the line of glory has possible connections with pagan cultic elements. As a result of marriages with pagan princesses the cult of pagan gods would have been introduced at court and consequently found a place in Jerusalem. One can argue that we also find this line of glory in Catholic spirituality. We find the same elements there. One example of this is the recent book by Boff about sacramental thought.[1] In this book he begins from a particular experience of reality, reality experienced as being transparent, transparent to the transcendent. Images and sacraments therefore play a major role in this book. Here Christ is the sacramental climax. Boff is concerned with traces of glory; he stresses Fortmann's view, that the invisible can be seen.[2] The basis of the book is a natural theology. Festivals play a major role. Erikson's notion that in religion the rites maintain contact with the mystery is confirmed here.[3] This line is concerned with a particular way of experiencing God's presence. But this presence is always elusive, just as the mother is not always present in contact with the child. Here I am thinking of Schillebeeckx.

Two things are possible here. First, as a result of the elusiveness of God's presence people slowly lose their faith in it and drift into indifference, or even into agnosticism. People are content with life in the 'they'. That is one possibility. The other is that they try desperately to hang on. In our day we can also see a Roman Catholic fundamentalism; a figure like the Dutch Bishop Gijsen is a clear instance of this. As a reaction to the void, these fundamentalists cling to the form, to the rite, to obedience. All this is as it were the most important thing, more important than the content. I would make two observations here. First, that we also find this line of glory and of the eye in the New Testament. We can argue that the Gospel of John is an example of this kind of spirituality.

Secondly, this line probably has its origin in relationship to the mother. Vergote's observation that the availability of God represents a maternal aspect over against the stress on law and authority, the paternal features, points to this.[4] It is also important that on this line of glory images have major significance. The French psychologist Jacques Lacan puts forward the interesting argument that in its relationship to the mother the child lives in an 'imaginary' order, in an order of imagery, and has not yet achieved discursive thinking.

The third way is that of Protestant spirituality. Terrien has rightly shown that alongside the line of glory in Israel there is also a line of the name. This line is more at home in Jewish spirituality than that of glory. On this line hearing, the ear, is central and all the emphasis lies on the significance of the word. Terrien points it out in the stories about the revelation on Sinai, and he also shows its influence in the northern part of Israel. There it is connected with the prophetic tradition and also gives a clear colour to the history of the Jewish people. On this line there is also a clash between Jewish piety on the one hand and the piety in the surrounding Near Eastern religions on the other. Within Christianity we find this line in what we can call Protestant spirituality. One example of this is Calvinism, and within Calvinism the theology of Karl Barth. In Barth's theology the Word of God is central: Christ is seen as the word of God. This spirituality is less attached to John than to Paul. The important thing is that it has a kind of elusiveness of its own which is based on the transcendence of God. In this spirituality God is the invisible one: there are no images of him nor may any images be made of him. As Levinas says, only traces of him may be seen. We may also say that God can be experienced in an indirect way. He can be experienced in Judaism in the Torah and the exposition of the Torah, and in Christianity in the Bible and the exposition of the Bible. As I have already indicated elsewhere, in a remarkable article Levinas argues that people can and must love the Torah more than God.[5] By this he means that they can then experience God better, that they can undermine as it were the elusiveness of his strength.

God can also be experienced indirectly in the celebration of festivals. There are certain festivals which play a major role in this spirituality. These are the festivals which recall the moments at which people have experienced God in the past, in other words recollections of the traces of God in history. Narrative theology, a theology the development of which is attracting attention at present, argues that in doing theology one must tell stories and in this way as it were retain the great recollections. So at certain Jewish festivals the story of the exodus from Egypt is told. In Christianity there are also festivals which recall the way in which

God once acted in history, like Christmas and Easter. Through the celebration of these festivals the void into which we look is overcome and the elusiveness of God is also robbed of its force. We experience in an indirect way that God is or has been present. At the same time these festivals are community festivals; the people, the family celebrates a festival. Well known images are the Seder evening for Jews and the celebration of Christmas for Christians.

Two observations need to be made here. First, that this spirituality has its roots in relationship with the father, the father-king. Kierkegaard speaks of a qualitative distance between human beings and God. This is the distance that there is between the subject and the king. Therefore in this spirituality the emphasis is on the elusiveness of God, as Terrien describes it. This father-king is the one who cannot be reached, the transcendent one, the one who approaches human beings with an authority from another world. He is the royal lawgiver. The second observation is that this relationship to the father-king is in tension with the relationship to the mother, just as the line of the name is in tension with the line of glory. Terrien describes how the prophets came into conflict with the temple, and we later see Protestantism in conflict with the Catholic mother church. Lacan says that the father in the family introduces a division into the relationship between mother and child. In Jewish families we see that after a particular period in which the relationship to the mother is dominant, the relationship to the father begins to dominate that to the mother. However, this does not meant that there is a complete opposition between the two; there is an implicit connection: a child's relationship to its mother forms a basis for its relationship to the father. The basic trust that the child receives in its relationship to the mother is also the basis for its relationship to the father. There is thus a unity with two poles. At the great festivals, moreover, we see the unity in tension. At these festivals God is on the one hand experienced with deep feelings of belonging and on the other in the awareness that as insignificant people we need to obey his royal law.

Two negative reactions are also possible within the framework of this spirituality. First of all, people can let go of God. This letting-go happens through breaking with him, in a kind of rebellion. Among Protestants we usually see a form of unbelief emerging, a deliberate choice of atheism. For them it is less a matter of drifting into agnosticism, as we find in Catholic spirituality. The other negative reaction is that people try to hold fast to their faith and the church in an obsessive way. Alongside Catholic fundamentalism there is also a Protestant fundamentalism. It is striking that this is organized above all in movements like the Moral Majority. There a considerable stress is placed on morality, on law; people must observe the Ten Commandments and respect the sabbath.[6] It is also striking that people maintain particular theological theories, for example in connection with creation. I would regard this obsessive holding on as an attempt to fill the void and in this way to deprive elusiveness of its power.

To return to the image of our journey: we have thus arrived above the treeline. How shall we make further progress? First let us review our situation. Beneath us is the village; it can be seen clearly. The sight of the village evokes a degree of nostalgia in us, but it also gives us some confidence. We know that we have brought provisions with us from the village, that we bought our equipment there and that we also have companions on the journey whose home is in the village. Above us lies the summit, a summit which can sometimes be seen but is also often withdrawn from our sight. We have a desire to get to the summit or at least as close as we can. We may ask ourselves what we shall find there. I do not think that we shall find rest there. The summit is not a paradise; it is certainly no Nirvana. But we shall find there what Moses found at the summit. There he found God's 'other side', and there he found the compass that he got from God for men and women: the Law. So reaching the summit does not mean that we shall get a final insight into the mystery of life. It does not give us a deeper knowledge, a gnosis.[7] It means that we see a direction, receive a route, have a compass in our hands. So essentially life at the summit is just the same as life on the way there. But at the summit we have more of a view. There is more affinity among men and women and between them and creation. It is colder and stormier there, but there is also more sun, and there is also a wider view. That means that faith is not really a higher life nor a deeper knowledge, but that that we live more authentically, more fiercely, more generously, more openly. And that is the direction of our journey.

So now we are half way; we are on the way, above the treeline. We have seen that the confrontation with the great problems of human life takes place in the wood. There we are confronted with meaninglessness, with the problems of freedom, with death and isolation, the four great problems which Yalom discusses in his book. In short, we can say that there we are confronted with the abyss of life, with the gulf of suffering, with the void. Our journey above the treeline calls for us to hack out positions for standing above the abyss on the firm ground of the mountain. But we have seen even more. We have also experienced how we are journeying with others, how we are bound to one another by ropes. The others to whom we are joined give us some support: they strengthen our basic trust and at the same time are a call to us. They look at us and in their faces we are, as Levinas puts it, addressed by them. In this team in which we are roped together above the treeline, there are also guides, people who know the way, who can help and encourage us. And above all in this team there is the great guide, the leader, the one who has taken the responsibility for this journey, who watches over his flock like a shepherd. So our relationships to one another are particularly important for life above the treeline. I want to discuss that in rather more detail.

The others are the companions who have joined us from the village for the climb, others to whom we are bound by all kinds of ties, of family, people, church work that we do together. We are originally bound together in what Kohut called a matrix of empathy. In this matrix we found some confirmation, we experienced a certain order and we had some rest. The matrix brought as it were the maternal element into our existence. In the wood that we entered together, however, we have often lost one another; between us and the others there is an alienation and we have found ourselves isolated. There is often still a residue of how things used to be, but the security and order in which we live have been eroded and undermined. There are many tensions in our lives and everything is done in a rush; incursions of the 'they' have had their effect. And now we begin to see the others above the treeline with new eyes. Alongside our original companions on the journey there are new people from other villages, who are also on the way to the summit. We are bound to all these people in a sort of community of fate, and this community brings a degree of openness into our existence. We want to trust one another, we find support from one another. The team to which we belong revives the maternal element of the original group; it brings order and a degree of repose. Alongside it, others also show their faces and, as I said, these faces challenge us. The others are as it were a gap in our world. I am thinking of the pictures of suffering people that we see on television, of men and women, young and old, who are perishing from hunger and sickness. As we see these pictures we realize what it means that we are above the treeline as people bound to one another, that we are roped together, that we are all on a journey. Being together on a journey means depending on one another. People must hold on to one another and must help one another on the way.

Here we also get a view of what a contemporary, modern spirituality is. This new spirituality includes the fact that we are aware of a deep alienation, but also have a remnant of inner security and faith. And alongside that, we are aware of a call. A contemporary spirituality includes the fact that we human beings, roped together, are hacking out footholds in the mountain that we are climbing, on slopes on which we sometimes hang above sheer cliffs. It is important that we see that in this situation we have a disclosure, a disclosure of another reality. The small group, the group which is roped together, gives those involved a sense of security, a sense of nearness and thus encouragement. That means that within this small group the sense of another order arises, that same order which bound us to one another at home. This means that as men and women in this small group we give one another credit and that an elusive presence makes itself felt in it. In theological terms this means that this small group has something in it of the kingdom of God, of the Church (with a capital C). It is an *ecclesiola in ecclesia*. We find this small church in modern times in all kinds of training groups, in encounter groups and charismatic groups, and here and there in particular religious communities.

I believe that such basic groups, in other words groups which are taking shape at grass-roots level, are a reaction to the modern process of alienation and at the same time are a reaction to the harshness of life above the treeline. E.F.Schumacher[8] and Professor van Gennep[9] have written about the significance of the small-scale group.

Here the figure of the guide has a special function. People need a guide when climbing mountains. A guide knows the way, he has a compass and he can read the compass. He feels responsible for the group. He has so to speak made a contract with it: he takes responsibility for the success of the journey and in so doing he feels committed to those who have problems or who fall by the wayside; indeed he takes particular care of them. I think that this figure of the guide casts light on the figure of Christ. I want to make some comments about this.

In the first place, through the figure of the guide I am trying to express our faith in Christ. Here the stress lies first of all on his work. I am taking van Peursen's line and approaching the figure of Christ in functional rather than ontological terms.[10] Secondly, the function of Christ consists in his presence. In the Gospels all the emphasis is on the miracles which Christ does, and on the words that he speaks. Here, in these miracles and in these words, there is a disclosure of a special presence. So too the resurrection appearances are a disclosure of this presence. Here he represents (makes present) the reality of the kingdom of God. That means that he is the Messiah, the one sent by God. In his presence, his miracles and his words he sets the kingdom of God in motion and in so doing he represents the king-god of this kingdom.

The third thing that I want to note is that it is the function of the guide to direct the group towards the summit. In the context of the image of the mountain climb this is an inward movement, which comes about in confrontation with the void, the abyss. In this movement the group sees a way forward. It grows in trust, in community, in hope and in love. The function of Christ here is that he shows this way and leads the group on it, indeed where necessary goes ahead, even into the abyss. In Christ, therefore, as human beings we see the depth of life before us, but also the way upwards. At the same time Christ is an image for us of how we can keep together as a group. His function is to represent the elusive presence of God. That means that in Christ we experience God coming to us. However, he comes to us in such a way that questions are asked of our faith, in other words, that we are prepared and in a state to give him credit. In this way Christ in our group is the teacher, the prophet, the comforter and at the same time the martyr who sacrifies himself, the sacrificial lamb. He has two sides: on the one hand he is presence and on the other he is leader and lawgiver. In other words, he has both a maternal and a paternal aspect.

Contemporary spirituality

Finally we must think about the possibility of a contemporary spirituality. I hope that what I understand by spirituality has become clear. For me it is an expression of human life, the human quest. Our existence is characterized by a confrontation with the void. It is unthinkable without the elusive presence; from the beginning there is the void which arises through the disappearance of the mother and the father. This void remains present as a result of the disappearance of the protection of social life, the replacement of the matrix of empathy, and the disappearance of God. This means that people are constantly thrown back on themselves in the world. Now a contemporary spirituality is the answer of the person of today to this void. It is not a theoretical answer, but life lived in faith in the elusive presence. Men and women used to have the support of society for this belief; there were authoritative father figures, there was the sacred order and there was the presence of God in the church with its images, its sacraments, its rites. Thus spirituality used to be the internalization of what was externally present. It consisted in a struggle against superficiality, against self-love, against the externalization of life; one instance of that is Teresa of Avila's *Interior Castle*. In this spirituality inwardness is sought through meditation and prayer; here they really remain within the structures of the universal human pattern. They remain as it were in the village below, and from there have a view of the summit far away.

However, contemporary, modern spirituality is that of people who have got above the treeline. In other words, it is a spirituality of those who live without the support of the structures of society and are engaged in a personal quest. They do that in the context of a group, but the stress is on the personal dimension. It is also a search in which God is not obvious: God must as it were be found again.

In seeking for and finding God men and women come up against two great realities: on the one hand the reality of suffering and on the other that of our fellow human beings. Through these two realities they get a prospect of the summit. Their coming to believe in God means that they must as it were hack a way in the mountain wall in the face of these two realities. Here people need nourishment if they are to be able to cope. They find it in two important sources: the first is basic trust. That is what we have taken from the village of our youth. This basic trust is born in the first fundamental confrontation with the void, with being abandoned, with the void of life. Erikson in particular has opened our eyes to this.[11] The second source of nourishment is what we find in our lives as this basic trust is reactivated in later contacts. The group can form such a source, and sometimes also provides a therapy, in which men and women are involved. We human beings need a matrix of empathy to feed our personalities. A good example of this is what Bonhoeffer has written about the *disciplina arcani*, the celebration of the mysteries of faith in hiddenness;[12] there is food for our spirituality in the community, although for Bonhoeffer this is always related to the world. It is important for us to have rites in our spirituality. As we saw, Erikson has also made important comments on that.[13] We need these rites to reactivate the mystery of love in our life.

What can also be said about this spirituality is that it lives in celebration. This celebration has different aspects. In the first place it is an expression of community. In the second place the recollection evokes life. In celebration we remember our links with those who have gone before, above all with the martyrs and with the great guide: his teaching and his sacrifice. This celebration takes place in the eucharist, which reactivates the group's link with the one who has gone before us into the abyss. In the eucharist we celebrate his glory and we bear witness to our trust. It thus brings about a reactivation of the identity of the group.

In this celebration there is also the special aspect of the story: following the line of the name, the exposition of the story, we recall that we have been given a compass. We also find the two lines, that of glory, the priestly line, and that of the name, the prophetic line, in the present time. Here we see above all how the second line, the prophetic line, has now come more strongly to the fore. Liberation theology is an example of this. However, we must not forget that glory, the celebration of the bond between the group and the great guide in the eucharist, may not be neglected. If there is anything that we must say about a contemporary spirituality, it is that it must lead to an ecumenical spirituality, and that means a spirituality which connects both aspects, that of glory and that of the name.

Thus spirituality finds its expression in a certain praxis, a praxis which is characterized by the great words faith, hope and love. In short we can say that life in faith is a life in commitment, following a decision, keeping to it, giving credit. That means that we have begun our journey and that we resolve to go on with this journey. Our life-style is focussed on it. We are required to be ready to camp, to leave our secure house. We are also required to be ready to converse, constantly to consult the map together. We are also required to press on, in so doing supported by the resolve that we have taken in faith. Spirituality also flourishes in the practice of hope. We expect that we shall make some progress in life, that we shall be able to achieve something, that we are on the way towards wider spaces and greater light and that we therefore must not lose ourselves in a whole variety of trivia.

The third key word is love. This means that we keep close to one another on the journey. We know (and we also experience) that we constantly have conflicts, that there will be disruptions in our relationships and that we will irritate one another. But from this we shall often receive a call; we shall not let go of one another, but hold tight to one another. One can say that a contemporary spirituality is the morality of the group on its journey to the summit. If we think for a moment of the situation of such a group, we shall realize that it derives its support from what it sees ahead. It knows how hard it is to find a way above the treeline, but it constantly derives encouragement from the view of the top. That brings into the life of the group, and thus into that of the individual, a sphere of freedom which finds expression in humour and creativity, which constantly influence the atmosphere. In some of his books Kohut has said that where people return to the deepest source of life, they begin to live from humour and creativity. Both are essential components in an authentic life. They are also an expression of a deep joy.

NOTES

1. A View of the Summit

1. It is not easy to define spirituality. The term is often used in Roman Catholicism, hardly ever in Calvinism and sometimes by Lutherans. But there has been a growing interest in Protestant circles over recent years in what is denoted by the term spirituality, and so one finds the word increasingly used. It shows a desire for experience (religious experience) and even more a desire to give form to this experience in daily life. At a deeper level we find here a desire for the personalization and the deepening of religious life, a desire for authentic 'converse with God', a need to transcend the level of doubt and discussion on the one hand and the superficial effect of everyday life on the other (cf. Heidegger's 'they').

Spirituality is the answer to the question 'How do I experience myself (and how do I behave) as a believer?' Here it is important to note that in the sphere of such an experience of ourselves, i.e. the feeling we have about ourselves, we do not have sufficient detachment from ourselves to be able to speak of ourselves in the usual predicative way and therefore we have to search for images to clarify our identity (as believers) and our search for that identity. The famous writers on spirituality demonstrate this. Teresa of Avila uses the image of the interior castle, and John Bunyan that of the journey in his *Pilgrim's Progress*. So we can see that spirituality (and its imagery) is concerned with a particular experience of our identity as human beings and believers.

2. Martin Heidegger was Professor of Philosophy in Marburg and Freiburg. He was a pupil of Edmund Husserl and built on Husserl's phenomenological philosophy in his book *Being and Time* (1927, English translation by John Macquarrie, SCM Press and Harper and Row 1962, reissued Blackwell 1967), which can be regarded as one of the most important works of existentialist philosophy (twentieth-century philosophical thought about human existence). His later work, which consists more of essays, comprises a number of smaller studies which can be regarded as approaches to a new 'ontology'.

Other famous representatives of this existentialist trend in philosophy have been Karl Jaspers in Germany and Jean-Paul Sartre in France. This trend found an echo among many writers, above all in France, including Albert Camus.

3. The experience of God's absence (or presence), in the sense in which a number of radical theologians talk about it, has become a central fact for me, as will emerge in due course.

4. John Robinson was an Anglican bishop and New Testament scholar. His *Honest to God*, SCM Press and Westminster Press 1963, rapidly became an international bestseller; this shows that his radical questioning echoed a widespread uncertainty among many believers.

5. Dietrich Bonhoeffer (1906-1945) was one of the leaders of the church opposition in Germany to National Socialism and during the Second World War also joined the underground resistance; after the failure of the attempt on Hitler he was arrested, and he was executed shortly before the end of the war. In prison he wrote regularly to – and for – his friend Eberhard Bethge, who later became his biographer. Bethge collected this material, which includes a number of thoughts on the renewal of theology, in the book *Letters and Papers from Prison*. The latest edition, the Enlarged Edition, is published by SCM Press and Macmillan, New York 1971.

6. Heije Faber, *Psychology of Religion*, SCM Press 1976.

7. James E.Loder, *The Transforming Moment*, Harper and Row 1981.

8. Joachim Scharfenberg teaches psychology of religion at the University of Kiel. Horst Kämpfer is involved in religious education in Germany. The book indicates the significance of symbols for religious life.

9. H.Faber, 'Zicht op de structuur van de godsdienstige ervaring: twee boeken', *Nederlands Theologisch Tijdschrift* 36.4.

10. Ian T.Ramsey was a well-known English philosopher of religion and Bishop of Durham. His books include *Religious Language*, SCM Press 1956, and *Models and Mystery*, Oxford University Press 1964.

11. Samuel Terrien, *The Elusive Presence*, Harper and Row 1978. Samuel Terrien is Emeritus Professor of Old Testament at Union Theology Seminary, New York.

12. W.Eichrodt, *Theology of the Old Testament*, SCM Press Ltd and Westminster Press 1961, 1967; G.von Rad, *Old Testament Theology*, Oliver and Boyd and Harper and Row 1962, 1965, reissued SCM Press 1975 (each is in two volumes).

13. See my *Psychology of Religion*, 267-9.

14. Since Freud we have also realized the role which can be played by projections of parental figures of parents in building up an image of God. In my *Psychology of Religion*, I sometimes stopped at this point. In religions like Judaism and Islam, which stress the distance between God and human beings and which combine an opposition to imagery with a

stress on the word in relations between God and human beings, father projections play a major role.

15. See my *Psychology of Religion*, in which I put forward the hypothesis that the stress on the distant authority inevitably provokes a desire for his nearness.

16. See the article 'Meer van de Thora houden dan van God', in Levinas's collected essays, *Het menselijk Gelaat*, Utrecht 1969. In this article Levinas argues that the relationship between God and man is not a communion based on feeling (Judaism calls for trust in an absent God, a God who covers his face), but a relationship between spirits through education and instruction, through the Torah. God is made concrete through the Law.

17. According to most critics, moreover, the title of Albert Schweitzer's well-known book *The Mysticism of Paul the Apostle*, A. & C.Black 1956, is misleading.

18. Heije Faber, *Psychology of Religion*, 275-9.

19. For Vergote see above all Anton Vergote and Alvaro Tamayo, *The Parental Figures and the Representation of God*, The Hague 1981.

2. At the Foot

1. Early recollections usually emerge in veiled forms in dreams. One can get on the track of them through associations. In psycho-analysis dreams are thus the *via regia*, the royal way, to the suppressed unconscious. In psycho-analysis the analysis of transference (the feelings of the patient towards the therapist) also offers a possibility of some insight into the first human relationships.

2. For the first year of life see René A.Spitz, *Vom Säugling zum Kleinkind*, Stuttgart 1967.

3. The Oedipus complex is the complex of feelings of the (young) son towards his father. Freud clarified this complex by the legend of Oedipus, the young son of the king, who killed his father and went on to marry his mother.

4. In psycho-analysis, investigation of the so-called object relationship (object of love) is increasingly beginning to play a role, especially the relationship between the child and the mother. In Freud the stress was above all on the child's relationship to the father. Coupled with that is a development in the formation of psycho-analytical theory: from a theory of human drives and their structure (Freud) this develops through ego psychology (Hartmann) into a 'psychology of the self' (Kohut).

5. For Heinz Kohut's 'psychology of the self' see his books: *The Analysis of the Self*, International Universities Press, New York 1971; *The Restoration of the Self*, International Universities Press 1977; *The*

Search for the Self, International Universities Press 1978; *How does Analysis Cure?*, International Universities Press 1984.

6. For Freud religion is therefore an illusion, as he argues in his *The Future of an Illusion*, Hogarth Press 1962. It arises from the need of the child for a father who solves the riddle of life through his omnipotence and omniscience. The child in the human being projects the image of the father on to heaven.

7. See my *Psychology of Religion*, 150ff.

8. For Erikson's view of religion see *Young Man Luther*, Faber and Faber 1959, 263-6.

9. A.A.A.Teruwe is a woman psychiatrist in Nijmegen, who has made a special study of the problems in the first relationship of human beings and who introduced the concept of frustration neurosis. Her theories are close to those of Kohut; cf.*Geloven zonder Angst of Vrees*, Roermond 1970.

10. Freud talks about the army (and the church) in *Mass Psychology and Ego Analysis*, Chapter V, 'Two Artificial Masses: Church and Army'.

11. A good example of this is *Church Dogmatics* III.4, T.& T.Clark 1961, 366ff.

12. In his *Young Man Luther*, Erikson has shown the influence of a structured monastic life can have on a person during the years of spiritual growth.

13. For the role of Von Staupitz in the life of Luther see Erikson, *Young Man Luther*.

14. Regression in support of the ego is a well-known idea in psychoanalysis. It means that through a return to an earlier infantile stage in development the ego is in a position to gain strength or to be strengthened by moving towards inner growth.

15. At various points in her books Dorothee Sölle has expressed the idea that in order God has no other hands – to help human beings – than our hands. From a human point of view this means that in our help we make God present to others.

3. In the Darkness of the Wood

1. In various studies, as for example *Childhood and Society*, Hogarth Press 1964, and *Identity: Youth and Crisis*, Faber 1968, Erikson argues that in the very first phase of human development an essential basic trust must be gained in place of an equally fundamental mistrust.

2. For Harlow's animal experiments see my *Psychology of Religion*, 159 and the bibliography there.

3. So-called existentialist philosophy developed above all after the Second World War. For all the clear difference between them, its

representatives like Heidegger, Jaspers, Sartre, Camus and so on have in common the fact that they philosophize about human beings as they encounter them in this world, in particular without a prior view with a specific metaphysic. The climate of this existentialist thought is strongly determined by Kierkegaard and Nietzsche.

4. *Being and Time* is the work in which, in 1927, Martin Heidegger formulated the starting points for his existentialist thought.

5. Jean-Paul Sartre, the best-known representative of French existentialism, developed these ideas in summary form in his short book *L'Existentialisme est un Humanisme*. They also form the starting point for his *magnum opus Being and Nothingness*, Methuen 1957.

6. Nietzsche included his famous essay 'The Madman', the man who ran through the city crying 'God is dead', in his book *The Joyful Wisdom*, Allen and Unwin 1937.

7. In his book *Om het eeuwig Goed*, H.T.de Graaf has given a description of religion as the human quest, and of finding one's place in the inexhaustible bond of life.

8. Emmanuel Levinas, who was born in Lithuania in 1906, is one of the most important contemporary French philosophers. His main work is *Totalité et Infini*, published in 1961. The significance of Levinas seems to me to lie in the fact that through the thesis that in the relationship between human beings there is an ethical call with a metaphysical depth he indicates new ways of thinking about human beings which in existentialism seem to be trapped in immanent categories.

9. Heidegger writes clearly about 'thrownness' and its significance in *Being and Time*, 399f.

10. For the concept of care in Heidegger see *Being and Time*, 225ff.

11. For being human as a burden see *Being and Time*, 173.

12. For Heidegger the 'they' is an essential concept which determines all his thinking about being human. See 163f.

13. Heidegger writes about 'distancing' in *Being and Time*, 164.

14. For the relationship of human beings to death see *Being and Time*, 279ff.

15. Heidegger gives extended accounts of the 'self' and 'authenticity' in *Being and Time*, 312ff.

16. In the collection *Pour un nouvel Humanisme*, in which an account was published of the Rencontres Internationales de Génève of 1949, one can find in one of the discussions a comment by Karl Barth that he is not fond of drawing a line between believer and unbeliever ('C'est un certain Karl Barth, qui est cet autre, qui ne veut pas croire').

17. See especially Irwin D.Yalom, *Theory and Practice of Group Psychotherapy*, Basic Books 1975; id., *Existential Psychotherapy*, Basic Books 1980.

18. Camus is famous for a number of essays and novels like *The Myth of Sisyphus*, *The Stranger*, *The Fall*, *The Plague*, *The Rebel*.

19. John Le Carré, *The Little Drummer Girl*, Hodder 1983.

20. W.Brede Kristensen (1867-1953) was Professor of the History and Phenomenology of Religion in the Theological Faculty at Leiden from 1901 to 1937. His best known publications are: *Het Leven uit de Dood*, *Verzamelte Bijdragen tot Kennis der antieke Godsdiensten*, *Symbool en Werkelijkheid*, *Inleiding tot de Godsdienstgeschiedenis* and *The Meaning of Religion*, The Hague 1960. He was a great expert in Egyptian and Greek religion.

21. Han Fortmann (1912-1970), Professor in Cultural Psychology and Psychology of Religion in Nijmegen, was a well known leader in the emancipation of Roman Catholics at this time. His main work is his study *Als ziende de Onzielijke*, in three volumes, published in 1964ff.

22. Heidegger wrote a significant article on the significance of technology entitled 'Die Frage nach der Technik', *Vorträge und Aufsätze*, Pfullingen 1954. I discussed this article in my *Psychology of Religion*, 223ff.

23. This aspect of Marxism can be seen most clearly in the Communist Manifesto, published in 1848, the year of revolution.

4. Reading the Map

1. The experience of the void is a primal religious experience. Compare for example the book that I have already mentioned by James E.Loder, *The Transforming Moment*. This experience has deep significance among many mystics. One finds some psychological clarification of this in Kohut's book about the earliest child-mother relationship.

2. Robert A.Nisbet, *The Sociological Tradition* (1946), Basic Books 1967.

3. Han Fortmann, *Wat is er met de Mens gebeurd?*, Utrecht 1961.

4. Jo Boer, *Dorp in Drenthe*, Meppel 1975.

5. The village of Montaillou is brought to life in E.Leroy Ladurie, *Montaillou*, Penguin Books 1980.

6. Jan Romein, an Amsterdam historian, developed the idea of the universal human pattern in a number of his books. This universal pattern comprises a number of features which are common to the cultures of the pre-industrial world.

7. Arnold Gehlen, *Die Seele im technischen Zeitalter*, Hamburg 1957. Gehlen was a German sociologist who was extremely important for his study of the influence of various cultural patterns on human society.

8. See Jo Boer, *Dorp in Drenthe*, 284f.

9. Paul Tillich, *The Courage to Be*, Fontana Books 1962.

10. Heidegger wrote about 'Lichten', etc., in an article about Heraclitus

entitled 'Aletheia', in the collection *Vorträge und Aufsätze,* Pfullingen 1954, and in *Über den Humanismus,* 15-20. For Jaspers cf. for example what he writes about 'active contemplation' in *Philosophie* II, *Existenz-hellung,* Berlin 1956.

11. Abraham Maslow, one of the leading figures in the sphere of psychology, became known above all through his theory of personality, in which he emphasized the aspect of growth, which is advanced on a scale of needs. In this growth, peak experiences, both religious and non-religious, play an important role.

5. Above the Treeline

1. Karl Barth's comment 'religion is unbelief' is famous. By it he meant that religious feelings and activities, in other words the human side of religion, contrast with the essential element of belief, which consists in an existential decision. If I understand this rightly, we have here a parallel to what Heidegger means by calling people back from escaping (from authentic existence, confrontation with nothingness) into the everyday-ness of the 'they'.

2. A deeper analysis of the reports on the experiment that the Theological Faculty in Tilburg carried out in connection with the diocese of Den Bosch between 1976 and 1982 shows that existential questions play a major role at a deeper level.

3. Tjeu van de Berk (1938) is a lecturer in catechetics at the Catholic Theological High School in Amsterdam. After his dissertation *Bonhoeffer, boeiend en geboeid,* 1974, he has written two further books: *Vluchten kan niet meer,* Antwerp and Amsterdam 1979, and *Opvoeden in geloven,* KRO Hilversum 1980.

4. William Hamilton, *The New Essence of Christianity,* Association Press, New York 1966, 24-6, quotes with approval the Italian writer Ignazio Silone, who compares the spiritual situation of our time with life in a displaced persons' camp.

5. In the lives of Kierkegaard and Nietzsche, who can be regarded as the forerunners of modern existentialism, there is a stress on individuality and on the search for their deepest identity in it. In *Being and Time,* Heidegger writes: 'Dasein is authentically itself in the primordial indivi-dualization of the reticent resoluteness which exacts anxiety of itself' (369).

6. Edward Schillebeeckx, *God is New Each Moment,* T.&.T.Clark and Seabury Press 1983, 127f.

7. Cf. e.g. Dietrich Bonhoeffer, *Letters and Papers From Prison. The Enlarged Edition,* SCM Press and Macmillan 1971, 'God would have us know that we must live as men who manage our lives without him' (360).

8. Herman Wiersinga, *Verzoening met het Lijden?,* Baarn 1975.

9. Cf. Albert Camus, *The Myth of Sisyphus*, Penguin Books 1975, and *The Rebel*, Penguin Books 1974.

10. Edward Schillebeeckx, *God is New Each Moment*, 108.

11. Dorothee Sölle, *Leiden*, Kreuz Verlag 1973, 54f.

12. William Hamilton, *The New Essence of Christianity*, 43f.

13. Barth, Berkhof and Schillebeeckx are three theologians in whose writings one can find conflicting interpretations of the saying 'My God, my God, why hast thou forsaken me?'

14. One can perhaps argue that guilt and reconciliation – within the framework of patriarchal society and the relationship between God and humankind which is intrinsically bound up with that – has been the central theme of Western theology: there is a clear line from Paul through Augustine, Anselm and the Reformation to Karl Barth, with a parallel in Roman Catholic theology and faith. Hamilton is right in observing that the problem of suffering has never been a central theme as a result. One of the consequences of this seems to be that the problem of guilt is now raised in a different way, less as guilt about the punishing and reconciling God and more as guilt about oneself or the other and through that about God.

15. This phrase was used by Tillich in a 1926 article, 'Die religiöse Lage der Gegenwart'.

16. Willard R.Sperry, *Religion in America*, Harvard University Press 1946, a study of religion between the two World Wars, demonstrates that at that time death was suppressed in public life in the United States. It can be said that this was true of many Western countries with a bourgeois way of life. Agatha Christie gives a good example of this in her autobiography.

17. In his *Existenzhellung*, Karl Jaspers develops the idea of boundary situations in human existence: these are historical conditioning, death, suffering, disputes and guilt, and there is also the 'questionability' of all existence and the historicity of the real.

18. The VELKD ('Vereinigte Evangelisch-Lutherische Kirche Deutschlands'), a federation of the German Landeskirchen, has a 'seminary' of its own, a centre for reflection and training, in Pullach near Munich. The course I refer to was held there and lasted six weeks; it was on 'The anthropology of those who suffer' and dealt with the religious problems of suffering in an interdisciplinary connection.

19. In her book on suffering Dorothee Sölle devotes a good deal of attention to the positive significance of the expression of suffering (see especially *Leiden*, 56ff.); this is a notion which also underlies modern pyschotherapy.

20. There has been much study of the effect of psychotherapy. Results suggest that the quality of the relationship between the therapist and the client is the most important factor.

21. Carl Rogers, the American clinical psychologist, became very influential in Europe after the Second World War as a result of his so-called non-directive psychotherapy, in which he put much stress on the quality (authenticity) of the feelings in the relationship between therapist and client.

22. In an article in *Het menselijk Gelaat* entitled 'Raadsel en Fenomeen', Levinas writes about the trace of God which he connects with the 'Lichtung' of which Heidegger writes, but also distinguishes the two (see pp.206f.). May one say that just as for Levinas 'the face can only appear as a face when it comes in a mysterious way from the Infinite' (206), for Sölle the hands of one's fellow human being can be experienced as God's hands? If I understand p.207 correctly, that means not as 'Lichtung', as a particular form of presence, but as the 'trace left by God'. In my view this does not exclude the possibility that psychologically there is an 'experience of' presence (in the sense of the reactivation of a recollection).

23. I have taken the term paradigm from Thomas S.Kuhn, *The Structure of Scientific Revolutions*, Chicago University Press 1962, a book which shows how the progress of science is through particular schools or trends which adopt particular paradigms.

25. So I think that one could speak of a messianic paradigm which gives place to a trinitarian-ontological paradigm.

26. One can say that Dorothee Sölle, *Christ the Representative*, SCM Press 1967, and Cornelis van Peursen, *Hij is het weer*, Kampen no date, are engaged in introducing a functional paradigm to replace the ontological one.

6. On with the Guide

1. Leonardo Boff, Los Sacramentos da Vida e da Vida dos Sacramentos, Vozes, Petropolis 1975.

2. Han Fortmann, *Als ziende de Onzienlijke*, Hilversum 1964, is built up on the notion that there is a religious perception of reality which is attacked by scientifc perception.

3. Erik H.Erikson, 'Ontogeny of Ritualization', in *Psychoanalysis – A General Psychology. Essays in Honour of Heinz Hartmann*, writes about the significance of rites in human life. Human beings give fixed form to their relationship to the holy mystery in their existence first in relationship to the mother and later in that to God.

4. For the availability of the mother see Anton Vergote and Alvaro Tamayo, *The Parental Figures and the Representation of God*, The Hague 1981.

5. For this article see Chapter 1, n.16 above.

6. It seems to me typical of Protestant fundamentalism that so much

emphasis is placed on the problems of morality and the significance of law in the Bible.

7. For the place of Gnosticism in the ancient world see Peter Brown, *The World of Late Antiquity*, Thames and Hudson 1971. The Dutch scholar G.Quispel has written a good deal about Gnosticism.

8. E.F.Schumacher, *Small is Beautiful*, Abacus Books 1973.

9. F.O.van Gennep, Professor of Theology at Leiden, defended the view that the church has its basis in the local (small) community.

10. Van Peursen's views are connected with his theory that mythical, ontological and functional phases can be demonstrated in the development of culture. I have written about this in my *Psychology of Religion*, 290-2.

11. In *Young Man Luther*, Erikson puts forward the view that human beings first discover (or rediscover) basic trust through a 'rock bottom' experience.

12. Compare what Bethge writes about the *disciplina arcani* in his biography *Dietrich Bonhoeffer*, Fount Books and Harper and Row 1977, 785-9.

13. For Erikson's article see n.3 above.